FLAVORS OF OAKLAND

A COOKBOOK IN 20 STORIES

WORDS BY ELAZAR SONTAG · PHOTOGRAPHS BY ANYA KU

Preface by Oakland Mayor Libby Schaaf · Foreword by Charlie Hallowell

Dedicated to Christopher Banes Walcott

Original text and cover design by Kerry Tremain, Berkeley, California

Revised text and cover design by Irene Rietschel, Albany, California

Printed in China on FSC certified paper

ISBN 978-0-9644352-7-8

TABLE OF CONTENTS

ACKNOWLEDGMENTS

It really does take a village. This book would not be what it is without the belief, love, and support of our community, and we would never have seen it grow into something really special without strangers showing their support as well. Thank you to all of our friends who have pushed us to keep going and shown confidence in our abilities.

The emotional support of our parents has been crucial during some of the tougher days, and we have enjoyed so much celebrating the successes with you. Jerry and Lorelei, my parents, put an immense amount of time into this book. They helped go over draft after draft of each story, and for that we are both so grateful. Without this assistance I would not have been able to develop my voice as a writer the way I have. Marco, Anya's father, donated rides around town. Maria, Anya's mother, walked us through our financial obligations. Every single receipt and invoice had to be filed away. She guided us around any tripwires and made sure everything we did was documented.

This book's creation was funded entirely by a crowdfunding campaign. More than 150 funders pooled their resources together and supported us. We are so excited to say your money went to all the right places. You made it possible for us to donate copies of **Flavors** to libraries, youth organizations, and other interested community groups. For a project like this, every dollar really did make a difference.

When we realized this project had grown wings and was going to need a real book designer, Kerry Tremain came to the rescue. The creative effort and time he put into the overall feel of the book is so appreciated. We owe him many home cooked meals. Kerry moved to Washington in the fall, and Irene Rietschel, another wonderful designer, took over to add her own aesthetic and bring the book home. Thank you Irene, you put the ribbon on the box.

We must acknowledge and thank the wonderful teachers and mentors who believed in us and supported us at every step of the way. And when the book was in its final stages, Mayor Libby Schaaf and restauranteur Charlie Hallowell contributed lovely pieces for the front of the book. Your thoughtful words were both encouraging and hugely helpful in raising interest in our project. Thank you to the other restauranteurs as well as founders and managers of grassroots organizations who wrote blurbs for the book.

Our friends at Paulding & Company, a team building kitchen in Emeryville, were kind enough to let us use their top of the line kitchen and supplies during recipe testing. They were very patient with us, even when things got a little messy. While testing recipes, a huge group of friends, young cooks, and mentors came to help. A special thanks to Samantha Smith and Sarah Wilson-Leech, both of whom spent many late nights in that kitchen testing and re-testing recipes.

Lastly, thank you to each and every one of the cooks who agreed to be a part of this book. You brought it to life. Many of the events you recounted to us at your dinner tables were not easy. We are humbled that you trusted us and we are honored to include you in this book. As we unwrap the first copies of **Flavors**, we will have you in mind, excited to share the product of this past year's hard work with you all.

PREFACE

THERE ARE SO MANY INGREDIENTS that go into making Oakland Oakland. I like to call it our secret sauce. I can't give away the whole recipe, but I can tell you it's a dash of gritty industrial flavor, a blend of opinions, backgrounds, and ideas (that we like to serve up choppy and smooth), and a heaping helping of creativity, passion for justice, and soul. Authentic and all natural—that's Oakland. No artificial flavors or colors added.

Oakland's fresh, made-to-order vibe is best exemplified by two things—our young people and our food. So it's not surprising at all that two Oakland-raised young people, Anya and Elazar, have cooked up *Flavors of Oakland: A Cookbook in 20 Stories*. Like master mixologists, they have married rich storytelling with beautiful photography to capture Oaklanders' love of coming together around a good meal—to honor the families, food, and cultural traditions that have shaped each of us and made us vital elements of the special brew that is Oakland.

It's also fitting that the creation of this book mirrors in many ways the making of a good old-fashioned potluck meal—with family, friends, and other proud Oaklanders contributing to the process of bringing this work of art to life. It's my honor to have been invited to be a part of the mix.

What you will find in *Flavors of Oakland* are mouth-watering recipes and even richer stories that will make you hunger to learn more about the people who call Oakland home, and what a tremendous place it is to live. With this effort, Anya and Elazar have shown how Oakland offers a combination you can't get anywhere else, so I definitely have to add a few more ingredients to the Oakland secret sauce recipe:

2 passionate, young Oaklanders with a fierce love of their hometown
20 of Oakland's 400,000 unique stories
1 captivating and filling read.

With Oakland-love,

Libby Schaaf
Mayor of Oakland

FOREWORD

I HAVE BEEN COOKING FOOD FOR PEOPLE IN OAKLAND for almost 20 years! I never thought I would settle here, and I never planned to find myself so entrenched in the Oakland food scene, but here I find myself, and almost every day I wonder at the luck of it. Oakland is an amazing city, a soulful city, and a complex city. It is filled with more different kinds of people than almost any other city in America, and on top of that it is awash in delicious food. We are surrounded by remarkable organic farms, farmers' markets within a short drive almost every day, and delicious restaurants in every little neighborhood. To grow up in Oakland, as my two kids have, is to grow up surrounded by flavor, by a diverse world of food: Ethiopian, Korean, Vietnamese, the best taco trucks in the world, and a growing number of chefs from all over the country who have decided to call Oakland home.

I first met Elazar at the Berkeley Farmers' Market working for Riverdog Farm. He was young and precocious, and falling in love with food. Every Saturday he would help all the local chefs pack up their produce, and ask questions about what they were cooking. He engaged and questioned, and before long he was working as an intern at my restaurant, Pizzaiolo. At the time I had no idea he was hatching a plan to write a book about Oakland food, but when Anya presented the book plan to me almost a year later it made so much sense. These two young Oakland food lovers wanted to dig a little deeper into the world of food they had grown up with all around them, and they wanted to share it with a larger audience. The combination of Anya's photographs and Elazar's stories is engaging, delicious, and a beautiful portrayal of what Oakland offers.

Flavors of Oakland is a testament to their work, and to the food of Oakland. It is an exploration of the ways in which Oakland is one of the richest food cities in America, and an example of what two young people who have hearts filled with passion and bellies full of food can accomplish. It has been such a pleasure getting to know both of these young adults as they explore what it is to create something, to bring something to life that before was just a fantasy. What a thing to do! Like cooking a delicious meal, like writing a beautiful menu, the sweet moment when the individual mind moves toward creation. **Flavors of Oakland** is a gift of insight from the youth of Oakland to Oakland herself! Support it! Cook from it! Eat from it! It will give you a taste of this remarkable city through the eyes and words of two of its amazing young people!

Charlie Hallowell
Pizzaiolo, Boot & Shoe Service, Penrose

INTRODUCTION

OAKLAND CAN BE A VERY CONFUSING CITY. Families that have lived within its borders for generations will tell you it is the greatest city on earth. Some of these families have had ample opportunity to move elsewhere but have stayed through thick and thin. They have put their children through the public school system and believed in Oakland no matter what. Many people move to Oakland and fall in love, as we heard over and over throughout our conversations with cooks. Other people, some young, some old, want nothing more than to leave Oakland; and when they do, they do not look back. These groups exist in the same city. One group will point to the graffiti-covered buildings and run-down burger joints and tell you, "This is an Oakland landmark, this is important;"… the other group will say, "These buildings are rundown and dejected, why are they still here?" In some sense, both of these people are right. Oakland does have rough edges and sharp points. People have lost some of their closest friends and relatives in this city. It has not been an easy place for all to grow up and live. But the sharp edges are complemented by beautifully smooth curves, formed by more than 150 years of migration, revolution, and delicious food.

In a changing economy and a new age of technology, Oakland is often spoken of as the new San Francisco. There is nothing wrong with a lower crime rate, more upscale residences, and fancier restaurants. But while Oaklanders welcome positive change and development as much as anyone, they know renovations, remodels, and new movers can't begin to tell the stories of this city. The stories are engrained in the cracked sidewalks, the old store signs, the heaping tacos and burritos of Fruitvale and carefully baked pastries of Chinatown, the Victorian houses of West Oakland—and in people's home kitchens.

In the pages of this book are the stories and recipes of 20 Oakland residents. Each of these people recalled moments of shared love, pain, and celebration in Oakland. Oakland, like many cities, is fragmented at times, and communication even among neighbors can become strained. But families pull together and neighbors resolve their issues. They make each other food during mourning and plan block parties for celebrations.

The city is full of cracks and tarnishes, like any well-used valuable is. And in these cracks and overlooked corners of the city is part of the real infrastructure holding the pieces together—thousands and thousands of home cooks from around the world. These Oaklanders roam the fresh markets scattered across the city, looking to find just the right chili paste or the perfectly crisp daikon. These are the people featured in this book. We chose to focus on home cooks instead of restaurants. Of course Oakland's restaurants are some of the best in the world. But, as such, they are already duly represented.

We were both in school full-time during the creation of this book. At times it has been frustrating and near impossible to juggle all our to-dos at once. But every time we sat down for a meal and heard another story, the stress and anxiety were swept away. Some of our hosts were born and raised in Oakland. They spoke of a quickly changing city, and the trade-offs that come with a lower crime rate, like losing their neighbors to spiking rents. Others came from every continent, traveled every sea, and chose to settle and begin new lives in Oakland. As this book developed, so did we.

By the end of the school year, we were exhausted but more motivated than ever to continue collecting stories and recipes.

This project is the result of the pure and unadulterated love and respect we share for Oakland. Many nights we rushed home from school and exchanged our textbooks and calculators for camera equipment and notebooks. We met in the middle of the city, usually around Lake Merritt, and hopped on a bus heading wherever our next meal was being cooked.

Wherever we went, doors opened and warm faces greeted us. This is the message we hope to impart to every reader. Meet your neighbors, ask them over for dinner. Talk about more than your job and the weather. Hear a story of travel, adventure, and change. If an eighteen- and sixteen-year-old duo can do it, so can you.

Elazar Sontag
Oakland, California

HOW TO READ THIS BOOK

THIS BOOK IS A COLLECTION OF RECIPES from 20 of Oakland's home cooks. Each dish is accompanied by a set of photos and a short story that gives context and color to the dish you will be cooking. Each chapter aims to give a sense of what it is like to sit down for a meal with this person; he could be a neighbor, she could be a new friend. We found our contributors in every way imaginable. Explaining how we put together each of these stories will help you understand and enjoy the book.

After arranging a mealtime with a cook, we would scour the East Bay to find all of the ingredients necessary for the dish. Any spices or seasonings that are not easily available are given an italicized explanation at the top of the recipe, and a store location that sells the product is included. You can also refer to the Resources page at the back of the book, which lists the local markets and restaurants recommended to us by our cooks.

After finding the necessary ingredients to cook each dish, we would pack up our notebooks and camera equipment, and hop on the bus. On arrival we took note of the personality and character of the cook's neighborhood. The stories will give you an idea of what each neighborhood feels like on first visit, the immediate vibe of the area.

With arms full of groceries, we met our cooks, often for the first time. Although we were new to each other, and sometimes spoke little of the same language, we could understand each other through food. As we began to unpack groceries, and conversation shifted to the dish we were going to learn to cook, any discomfort dissolved. Whether you speak English or Mandarin, garlic is peeled and prepared the same way. In Spanish or Russian, onions must be chopped and tomatoes rinsed. We found an understanding through a universal language that broke down any barriers. The stories in this book resonate with that feeling, which we experienced over and over again.

Descriptions of the cooking process are interspersed throughout each story, because as accounts of hardship, celebration, and change unreeled and developed, our senses were simultaneously swimming in the aromas of fresh herbs, sizzling curry powders, and toasting spices.

You may notice the measurements and instructions for some recipes are looser than for others. This is a reflection of the cooking styles of different people and their cultures. Regardless of whether the onion you use for Jackie and Rebecca's curry is large, medium, or small, the curry will be delicious. Recipes that require more exact measurement have weight and cup measurements next to the ingredient name.

Feel free to change and develop these recipes in whatever way you please. Use the stories as a means to open conversation over your own dinner table, telling your stories as you prepare a meal and sit to eat. If you have been meaning to meet your neighbors but haven't quite done so, arrange a time to cook a simple lunch or dinner to share. There is no conversation you cannot start over a meal.

BLUE CHEESE SOUP AND LOGO MOMO

GRAND LAKE, OAKLAND   YANGKYI

Blue Cheese Soup is most likely not a dish you have heard of. Reserve all judgment until you have had the chance to enjoy a steaming bowl of what has become a favorite in our households. The slight earthiness given by the blue cheese pairs perfectly with a gentle kick of heat from whole jalapeños. With a side plate of Logo Momo—pan-fried and steamed bread—this is a dinner that is sure to impress even your most traveled friends.

KULLU MANALI, WHERE YANGKYI WAS BORN, is a small village in the mountainous region of northwest India. It is 1200 miles from Markham, the Tibetan town her family is from, and a long, long way from her home in the Grand Lake neighborhood of Oakland. Anya and I walked up the gently rolling hills that lead from Lake Merritt to Yangkyi's apartment, expecting to learn to make one dish and then sit and hear her story. Instead, we had an unexpected feast awaiting us.

With steaming food on the table and intricately decorated Tibetan rugs spread over the floors, Oakland seemed to disappear as we entered her apartment. Yangkyi had prepared traditional Tibetan fare for us: hand-pulled noodles in a warm full broth with deliciously tender boiled beef, and Sha Momo—the traditional Tibetan dumpling made with a thick hand-stretched dough and a hearty meat filling.

While we enjoyed the steaming broth full of chili paste and rich flavor, Yangkyi prepared us another treat, called Tsampa. In the high mountains of Tibet, barley is the

staple crop. In this dish it is roasted and ground into a flour, and mixed in a small bowl with Chata, a black tea, and fatty yak butter. Tsampa is the resulting paste. It sticks to every part of the mouth, reminiscent of very thick peanut butter. Yangkyi's husband, Tenzin, who helped translate from Tibetan when Yangkyi couldn't find the English word, told us he and Yangkyi wake at 6:30 every morning to eat this porridge before they leave for work.

Yangkyi is Tibetan and has never lived in Tibet. Her parents had to flee to India in 1959, when China occupied Tibet. When Yangkyi was seven, her family moved to a refugee camp in South India. In the camp, her family ate all their meals together. They did not have a refrigerator, and even those in the camp who did were careful not to leave anything in one for too long, because the power went out often. The family would never buy more than they could eat in three or four days.

Yangkyi worked and grew up in the camp, married, and had two children. By extreme good fortune, the family acquired an American visa and moved to the States. She, her husband Tenzin, and the children started a new life in Oakland. Although Yangkyi feels privileged to have access to hot water and electricity, there are things she misses about her old home. In India, Yangkyi would leave her door unlocked from the moment she woke in the morning until the moment she went to sleep. She knew all her neighbors, and it was not uncommon for people to wander into her home off the street and sit for a cup of tea. Yangkyi and Tenzin sadly explained that they have lived in their apartment building for four years and they don't know a single one of their neighbors.

When Yankgyi arrived in the Bay Area, she got a job as the nanny for a family living in the Oakland Hills. When Yangkyi saw how busy John and Kim were, and how little fresh food they had the time to cook, she offered to make dinner for them. They loved the dishes she prepared, and she has been cooking for them ever since. The family helped Yangkyi get acclimated to Oakland, teaching her how to drive and use a computer, and helping her find a place to live. John and Kim have helped Yangkyi feel at home since the minute she met them.

When we finished our unexpected meal, Yangkyi began to prepare the dish we were so excited to try. She stood over a cutting board in her traditional Tibetan apron, made of the highest quality fabric and adorned with a variety of colored stripes. First, blue cheese and flour were mixed to thicken and flavor the chicken soup. Next, the pan-fried bread went into a scaldingly hot pot while the soup simmered away. Yangkyi warned that the top of the bread pot could not be lifted until the exact moment the bread was finished and the steam had soaked into the moist dough. As you will discover, the soup and bread are both well worth the work.

Power outages won't affect the refrigerator anymore, but, given how delicious this food is, don't expect it to be packed away for leftovers.

With steaming food on the table and intricately decorated Tibetan rugs spread over the floors, Oakland seemed to disappear as we entered her apartment…

BLUE CHEESE SOUP

Yields 4-6 portions

Start the Logo Momo (see next spread) first and allow to rise while the soup cooks.

3 pounds skinless bone-in chicken thighs

1 large yellow onion, chopped roughly

2 teaspoons salt

2 cloves garlic, chopped finely

1 inch ginger, peeled and chopped finely

5 medium jalapeños, seeded and quartered lengthwise

2 large Roma tomatoes, chopped roughly

8 ½ ounces blue cheese

½ bunch cilantro, chopped roughly

2 tablespoons flour

Olive oil, for pan frying

DIRECTIONS

Cut each of the chicken thighs into three pieces lengthwise, one piece including the full bone. Cut the two pieces without bone in half the opposite way to make about 1 inch cubes.

Heat a medium heavy-bottomed pot over high heat, and add enough oil to coat the bottom. Add the onions and salt and sauté until onions are lightly browned (3-5 minutes). Add garlic, ginger, and jalapeños and cook until fragrant (5-6 minutes).

Add the tomatoes and chicken to the pot and stir to combine. Cover the pot and turn to medium heat. Simmer for 10 minutes.

While the pot is covered, combine the blue cheese and flour in a small bowl and mix with a fork until a paste is formed. Add cilantro and 5 cups of water to the pot, or enough to cover the chicken by about 1 inch. Return to a simmer. Add the blue cheese paste and stir slowly so as not to break the jalapeños.

The soup should have a creamy consistency. If it is too watery, combine another 1 tablespoon of flour with 1 tablespoon of water and mix into the soup. Turn the temperature to medium-low and simmer the soup for 20 minutes, uncovered.

Skim most of the fat from the top of the soup, leaving a little for flavor.

LOGO MOMO

Yields 7 buns

1 tablespoon yeast

1⅓ cups warm water

2 teaspoons sugar

1 teaspoon salt

1 tablespoon baking powder

4 cups all purpose flour + more for dusting

Olive oil, for pan frying

1 cup water, for steaming

DIRECTIONS

To start the Logo Momo, mix the yeast, warm water, and sugar and set aside for 10 minutes to bloom the yeast. Mix the salt, baking powder, and flour in a large bowl. Add the yeast mixture to the dry ingredients. Combine the mixture and turn out onto a lightly floured surface. The dough will be flaky and may crumble.

Knead the dough. If the dough is dry, flatten it out and sprinkle it with a few drops of water, fold and knead the water in. Return dough to the bowl and leave covered with a towel for 30 minutes to rise. During this time, the dough will become more soft and workable but will remain stiff. Do not be discouraged; it softens and becomes moist when steamed.

Divide the dough into 7 equal parts and roll each into a ball. Using your thumbs make an indentation in the middle of each dough ball. All the sides and the bottom should be of equal thickness.

Heat a large heavy-bottomed pot over medium heat, and add enough oil to coat the bottom. Place all the balls hollow side down into the pan and fry until the bottoms are lightly browned (1–2 minutes). Add one cup of warm water and let boil on high heat for 30 seconds before covering with a lid. Reduce heat to medium low and cook for 9 minutes. Without removing the lid, remove the pot from heat and let rest for 3 minutes. This allows the buns to detach from the pot without sticking.

Serve hot and steaming with soup.

LAWTELL GUMBO

FRICK, OAKLAND JOHNNY

Part of the joy you will find in making this rich and delicious stew are the smells that emerge as the aromatics develop and cook down. Every step, from slowly browning your roux over high heat to de-veining the shrimp and killing the crabs (assuming they are alive and fresh), requires you to really tend to your gumbo. You will certainly gain the respect of your Southern friends when they come over for dinner to find a pot of Lawtell Gumbo on the stove.

ON OUR WAY TO JOHNNY'S HOUSE, we realized we had forgotten to buy the flour that was crucial in making gumbo, the dish Johnny had offered to teach us to cook. By the time we realized our mistake, we were already deep into East Oakland, an area of the city that is not known for offering a large number of grocery stores. We went block after block searching for a store. We saw families talking and laughing in their front yards, taco trucks set up on street corners letting off the irresistible smells of sweet yellow onions and cilantro, but we could not find a grocery store. Finally we came across Mi Pueblo Food Center and we were back on track.

When we reached Johnny, we were more than half an hour late, but he greeted us with a warm smile. The smell of freshly baked pie wafted out of the kitchen. Inga, Johnny's wife, had just pulled a Key Lime Pie out of the oven. Her family was over to join us for dinner. Her father relaxed on a recliner in the living room while her mother stood in the kitchen admiring the beautiful pie that had just appeared. Johnny and Inga's two young sons sat and played with toys on the dining room floor.

Johnny is from the small town of Lawtell, Louisiana. As a child, he played under the house to avoid the sweltering sun. He and his siblings would clear away the

Gumbo was always a staple dish for Johnny growing up. On cold nights in Lawtell, it is on every table. Johnny's uncle would always say that it "tightens up your ribs." It could feed the family for a week…

spiderwebs and spend their afternoons and evenings shooting dice under the porch until the dinner bell rang. Johnny was 22 when he left Louisiana and moved to Maryland. Zydeco music—a genre that originated in southwest Louisiana and can be identified by its fast pace and use of instruments like the washboard and piano accordion—was quite popular in Maryland. It was easy for Johnny to stay connected to his Louisiana roots. Zydeco musicians and dancers, many of whom Johnny already knew, or got to know when they performed, were constantly making the trip from Louisiana to play music in Maryland's music halls. On one of these trips to Maryland, a musician friend asked Johnny to make him a classic Lawtell Gumbo, a reminder of home. On seeing how Johnny was making the gumbo, he told Johnny to stand aside so he could show him how to make it "like your momma makes it." After that, Johnny began to take the cooking of his hometown more seriously.

Several years later, Johnny made the move to California for the beautiful weather and Zydeco dance, which his friends assured him he'd still be able to find on the West Coast. The music and food of Louisiana have followed him, enriched his life, and built and fed his family.

Although all of the ingredients used in the gumbo can be found nearly anywhere, Johnny was proud to show us many of the ones he had either brought back to Oakland from Lawtell or made himself. His homemade ingredients included the sausage that added a huge depth of flavor to the pot, and his Johnny Boy Seasoning, a mixture he has concocted that captures the flavors from his hometown and which he hopes to start selling in Oakland soon.

Gumbo was always a staple dish for Johnny growing up. On cold nights in Lawtell, it is on every table. Johnny's uncle would always say that it "tightens up your ribs." It could feed the family for a week. Recently, Johnny's uncle passed and he went home for the funeral. Johnny and his family gathered over a huge pot of gumbo. They feasted on crawfish, corn, and potatoes while they celebrated the life of his uncle.

Johnny has lived in Oakland for 14 years, and believes that a community is built by individuals and their ability to do good. People in Oakland may be more likely to gather at a farmers' market, while those in Louisiana host butchering events, killing and roasting several pigs, but the foundations for a strong community are the same. He thinks the city will be made more positive if everyone leads by example, by walking their children to school and talking to their neighbors.

Although Johnny loves Oakland, there are things about the South that he misses. Growing up in his small Southern town, the whole neighborhood looked out for him and his seven siblings. When he goes back to Lawtell, people are excited to see him, and act as if no time has passed. This is an attitude Johnny tries hard to embrace and nurture in the Frick neighborhood of East Oakland. If you pass by Johnny on the street, expect to be offered a helping hand, a cold beer, and maybe a bowl of Lawtell Gumbo the way his family makes it—and, if the stars are aligned, a slice of Inga's Key Lime Pie.

LAWTELL GUMBO

Yields 10–12 portions

If you are not keen on killing and cleaning the crabs yourself, your local fishmonger will be happy to do so for you. Make a big pot of white rice to accompany the rich gumbo.

Gumbo

1 (3 ½ pound) chicken, broken down (see directions)

Johnny Boy Seasoning (alternate recipe follows)

4 quarts (16 cups) chicken stock

5 cloves garlic, peeled

1 large onion, chopped finely

1 green bell pepper, seeded and chopped roughly

1 red bell pepper, seeded and chopped roughly

1 stalk celery, sliced thinly

1 green onion, peeled and chopped into thin rounds

¼ bunch Italian parsley, stemmed, chopped finely

1 (1 ½ pound) smoked ham shank (taso)

Roux (recipe follows)

2 (½ pound each) andouille sausages, cut in ¼ inch pieces

1 pound shrimp, peeled and de-veined

2 (1 ½–2 pound each) crabs, quartered and cleaned

1 tablespoon white vinegar

2 teaspoons Crystal Hot Sauce

Salt and pepper

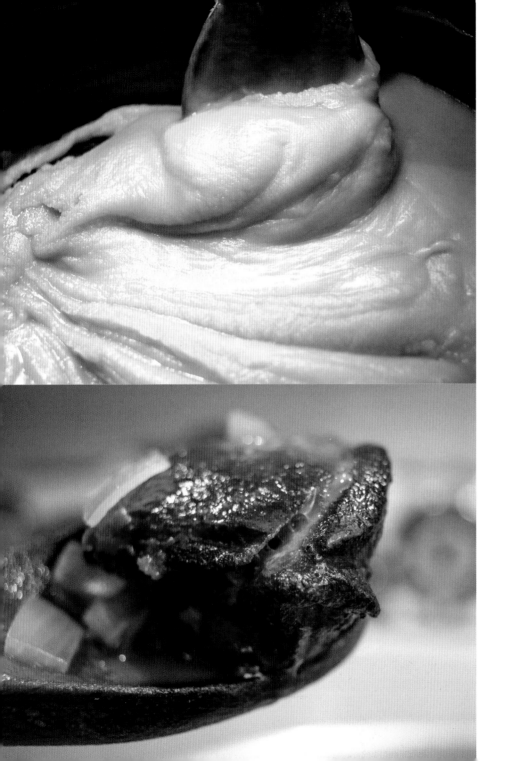

Johnny Boy Seasoning Alternative

2 teaspoons white sugar

1 teaspoon red crushed chili

1 teaspoon garlic powder

½ teaspoon hot paprika

¾ teaspoon sweet paprika

1 teaspoon ground white pepper

1 teaspoon ground black pepper

1 teaspoon salt

1 teaspoon ground thyme

Combine the seasoning mixture.

Roux

½ cup vegetable oil

1 cup flour

DIRECTIONS

Breaking down the chicken

Cut the breasts off of the bone with a sharp, flexible chef's knife or boning knife. Find the wing joint and cut the wing from the carcass. It is okay if this is slightly messy; all the meat is going into a soup pot and no one will be any the wiser. Pop the thigh out of its joint so you can find the connecting point and cut through it to separate the thighs from the carcass. When the carcass is clean, remove the skin from the breasts and thighs. Cut the breasts into 6 pieces each and the thighs into 3 pieces each, one including the bone.

Coat the chicken with the seasoning mixture and set aside.

In a large pot bring the chicken stock to a boil. Add the garlic, onion, bell peppers, celery, green onion, parsley, and smoked ham shank to the pot. Turn the heat to medium-low and simmer for 20 minutes, in which time you should begin the roux.

For the roux

Heat a large cast iron pan over medium high heat, and add the oil. Add the flour and stir constantly. Make sure to scrape the sides of the pot down so no flour burns.

When the roux starts to turn a caramel brown color and begins smoking, pull the pan from the heat and continue to stir rapidly. You may be convinced at this point that you have burnt the oil and flour mixture but this dark toasted roux is what gives the gumbo such a rich and delicious flavor.

When the roux has stopped smoking put it back on the heat. As the roux begins to smoke again, pull off heat again and stir. Continue this process until the roux has reached a dark chocolatey color (10-15 minutes).

Assembly

Pull the ham shank from the pot and begin to carefully spoon in the roux. Stir the mixture well to mix in all of the roux and be careful as you do this because the roux may splatter up as it hits the liquid. Chop the ham shank (discarding the bone) into ¼ inch cubes and return to the pot.

When the gumbo has thickened slightly and is bubbling slowly (5-10 minutes), add the chicken and andouille pieces. On medium heat simmer the gumbo for another 10-15 minutes, until the chicken is fully cooked when pierced with a knife. Add the shrimp and crab pieces. Cook until the shrimp is pink and the crab meat flakes when poked with a toothpick or skewer (5-10 minutes).

Add the white vinegar and Crystal Hot Sauce to bring a little more depth to the flavor in your pot. As the acidity gains a little, the other flavors will also become more balanced and noticeable.

Turn the heat to low. Scrape any foam off the top of the pot, and discard.

Finish with salt and black pepper. Serve over steaming white rice.

ROLLED TACOS, RICE, SALSA & GUACAMOLE

ROCKRIDGE, OAKLAND   MARTA

If you did not grow up in Mexico, you may be confused when it dawns on you that Marta's tacos do not look like the ones you see at taquerias—not like the tacos filled with rice and beans and meat and stacked high with toppings. These are the rolled tacos more commonly known as taquitos here in the States. Marta will indignantly tell you that these are tacos. Don't question it. As with many of the other recipes in this book, you may enjoy the cooking process most if you invite friends over. There are no complicated, head-scratcher steps, but there are lots of components. If everyone tackles one side dish, and someone cooks the rice, you will be eating before you know it.

MARTA LIVES IN A QUIET PART of the Rockridge neighborhood, in an area that informally marks the ending of city life. As I don't speak more then three words of Spanish, Anya, who is fluent in Spanish, did the preliminary introductions. I was most helpful as a handyman, reaching up to the top shelves to grab spices or utensils that lived higher than Marta could reach without a step-stool.

Marta grew up on Yusasino, a ranch in Oaxaca. While Marta's mother was cooking dinner, Marta and her six siblings were out on the farm with her father. Marta would plant corn, wheat, beans, and pumpkins. When she was not harvesting crops with her father or cooking with her mother, she was taking care of bees. Donning a plastic dry cleaners' bag to prevent bee stings, she would head out to gather honey from the 35 boxes on their ranch.

Donning a plastic dry cleaners' bag to prevent bee stings, she would head out to gather honey from the 35 boxes on their ranch...

On Mondays, Marta's parents would head to the neighboring town to buy groceries for the coming week. The kids would get into all kinds of mischief: taking jars of honey, picking the sweetest corn, and galavanting through the pumpkin fields.

Anything that they grew on the farm, they ate. Lima beans, corn, seven different grains, fresh tomatillos, peaches, almonds, everything ended up on their dinner table. Since the family did not own a grain mill, Marta would help prepare the wheat and corn that went into the evening tortillas, pounding them with a mortar and pestle. Before dinner, Marta would make the salsas. Since there was no refrigerator, everything was prepared fresh every day.

As she reminisced about her years on the ranch, Marta used her metal tongs to flip tomatillos and jalapeños on the cast iron skillet, where they smoldered and smoked, filling the room with a distinctly earthy aroma. Chicken steamed away in its poaching liquid, and toasted and golden rice lay covered in a heavy-bottomed pan where it absorbed the juices of the tomatoes.

For some time, the ranch did not have running water, so the children would bring water from the river to the house. A washboard was set up on the banks to clean their clothes, and it was here that they all bathed. There was a very old school on the ranch and all of the children attended it for several years. School was too expensive, so Marta began to learn things outside of school. She began to take classes in knitting and crocheting, learning to make everything by hand.

Then, at 17, Marta moved to a big town in Mexico. She continued to knit, and began to clean people's houses as a stable source of income. One of the clients she worked for had several restaurants, and offered her a job making coffee in the mornings. As the restaurant expanded, Marta started cooking there. Her days would sometimes go from dusk till dawn, cooking, cleaning, and working the register.

When she began to nanny for families, Marta put everything she had into the children. "The 11 kids that I nannied, they are everything. And I will always love these children. They are the loves of my life." One of these families moved from Mexico to San Diego, and she made the jump with them. In San Diego, Marta met a new family looking for help with their son, Oscar. Marta moved to Sonoma with the family, where they lived for several years, and then to Oakland, where she has lived across the street from them for the past 11 years. And as you would expect, her food principles followed her from the ranch—All the baby food she fed the kids, she made herself. For her 70th birthday, all the families Marta has worked for arranged a big dinner, giving her gifts and thanks for everything she has done for them over the years.

Although Marta has easy access to all the same ingredients here as she did in Yusasino, the flavors are not the same. Growing up, nothing was ever touched by a single chemical on their ranch. From the time her father planted a potato to the moment she or one of her siblings dug it up, all it ever came in contact with was the well-nourished soil. As she tells us about her past and the stories of her childhood, her youthful laugh and smile still paint a picture of a young Marta running through the fields with her siblings, stealing the sweetest ear of corn, and always coming home in time to make salsa for dinner.

ROLLED TACOS, RICE, SALSA & GUACAMOLE

Yields 9 tacos

Begin the guacamole and tomatillo salsa while the rice cooks so all the components are ready at roughly the same time.

Chicken

1 (¾–1 pound) large bone-in skin-on chicken breast

2 tablespoons salt

1 onion, peeled and quartered

1 clove garlic, peeled

⅓ bunch cilantro

Rice

5 large Roma tomatoes, chopped roughly

3 cups reserved chicken stock (from above)

2 cups long grain rice, rinsed and drained

1 teaspoon salt

⅓ bunch cilantro, stemmed

Olive oil, for toasting

Tomatillo Salsa

10-12 large tomatillos (1½ pounds)

2 small jalapeños, stems removed

¼ onion, chopped roughly

2 cloves garlic, peeled

1 tablespoon salt

⅓ bunch cilantro, stemmed and chopped finely

Guacamole

3 large avocados

2 small Roma tomatoes, seeded and chopped finely

¼ onion, chopped finely

½ small jalapeño, seeded and chopped finely

Salt

Tacos

1 package (9) corn tortillas

Shredded chicken (from above)

Olive oil, for frying

DIRECTIONS

For the chicken

Place the chicken in a medium pot, add enough water to cover, and turn to high heat. Add the salt, onion, garlic, and cilantro. When the water boils, turn heat to low and cover the pot. Boil the chicken until it can easily be pulled apart with two forks (30-45 minutes). Remove the chicken to a plate, strain the chicken stock, and set aside. When the chicken has cooled, remove skin and bone, and shred with your hands or two forks.

For the rice

In a blender or food processor, blend the tomatoes. Add enough chicken stock to make 5 total cups of liquid. Heat a medium heavy-bottomed pot over medium high heat, and add ¼ cup oil. When a grain of rice added to the pot sizzles and pops, add the rest of the rice and cook, stirring constantly until the first few grains of rice begin to turn brown and puff up slightly (5-6 minutes).

Add the 5 cups of tomato mixture, the salt, and the cilantro. Cover the pot and turn the heat very low. Cook for 40 minutes, remove from heat, fluff with a fork, and set aside.

For the salsa

Yields 3 cups

Remove and discard the husks from the tomatillos, and rinse the fruits until they are no longer sticky. Heat a large cast iron pan over high heat, and char the tomatillos and jalapeños, turning and rotating until all sides are black (8–10 minutes).

Add the tomatillos, jalapeños, onion, garlic, and salt to a food processor and process until all ingredients are well combined and the tomatillos are completely broken down. Refrigerate until cool, pour into a serving bowl, and garnish with cilantro.

For the guacamole

In a medium bowl mash the avocados roughly. Add the tomatoes, onion, and jalapeño. Add a large pinch of salt and taste. Balance accordingly.

For the tacos

Warm the corn tortillas in a large cast iron pan over high heat. Remove the tortillas to a plate and cover with a cloth towel to keep the steam in as you work. Put a small handful of shredded chicken in the middle of each tortilla. Fold the tortillas in half, fold the excess tortilla to one side and wrap underneath tightly.

Heat the large cast iron pan over medium heat, and add ¼ inch oil. Place the tacos in the pan with the folded side facing down to maintain the shape. Fry the tacos, turning until all sides are golden brown and crisp (6–8 minutes).

Remove the tacos to a plate covered with paper towels. Rest until any excess oil has drained.

Assembly

Place several tacos on a dinner plate with a heaping spoonful of rice and a generous serving of guacamole. Top everything with tomatillo salsa, and enjoy.

KULWA AND HAMLI

EAST LAKE, OAKLAND   ZIMAM

For those unfamiliar with Eritrean or Ethiopian food, you will be surprised by some of the flavors in these recipes. Spices like corrorima are likely to be new to the American palate; its flavor falls somewhere between mint and cardamom. As neither of these recipes will take very long, you'll have plenty of time to sit down around the table with your friends and family, a huge part of traditional Eritrean mealtime.

CAFE ERITREA D'AFRIQUE is a small Eritrean restaurant nestled in between a 99¢ discount store and a spiritual supply store. The lunch buffet sign hanging below the restaurant's red awning pulls in regulars who live in the Temescal neighborhood, and those who come from further afield to enjoy the traditional fare. Zimam, who lives in the East Lake neighborhood of Oakland, is the owner of the restaurant.

She learned to cook from her mother in Eritrea when she was little. It was traditional for the mother to teach the daughters to cook, something Zimam was especially keen on, as she was always interested in food. The Eritrean meal is almost always a shared one. Injera, a fermented and spongy flatbread, is laid on a big platter and all the foods that are being eaten are placed around the perimeter of the plate on top of the bread. Everyone sits down together to eat from the platter and check in about their days. It is unheard of to take a plate to your room.

Inside the restaurant, one of several patrons is always sitting at the bar or a nearby table, drinking dark strong coffee by day and switching to an Eritrean or Ethiopian brewed beer as the sun begins to set. These regular diners are likely to help you when

you walk in, kindly deciphering the choices on the menu, or even getting up to get you an extra napkin when it becomes apparent you do not know how to eat injera properly.

Our lack of knowledge seemed to grow as Zimam began cooking. We could not identify many of the spices in small metal containers on the countertop. Between us and the doorway bubbled a pot of onions so large it almost scraped the exhaust fan above. Below to one side was an enormous vat of house-made Eritrean spiced butter.

Zimam grew up in the midst of a civil war between Eritrea and its controlling power, Ethiopia. When she was very young, her father passed away and her mother raised their four children on her own. Starting when Zimam was 13, she and her siblings were in and out of school, depending on where the war was, unsure of what would happen next. When Zimam was 21, the whole family moved to Sudan. They lived there for five and a half years.

Zimam's brother moved to Oakland, and then sponsored her to follow behind him. There are still things she misses about her country. There was always a sense of community in Eritrea, despite the war. Zimam's parents never had to worry about whether she would eat well away from home. Zimam has formed a community similar to this with many of the neighboring restaurants in the area. It is not quite the same, since everyone is caught up in the rush of American life, but she makes an effort to stay connected, to slow down enough to sit for a cup of coffee and a shared plate of food with a friend or neighbor.

When asked where her favorite place in Oakland was, Zimam replied, "Asmara," another Eritrean restaurant only a few blocks from her own. She explained to us that her community does not share the competitive attitude of so many other restaurants.

When any of the local Ethiopian and Eritrean restaurants are out of spices, they call upon each other, and someone is bound to come over with whatever they need. On a peaceful day, any one restaurant owner is likely to be found relaxing at one of their sister restaurants.

Zimam started off at Cafe Eritrea in a very different position than she has now. Three weeks after moving to Oakland in 1991, she found a job working at the restaurant, beginning as a dishwasher. Zimam began to notice that the cooks were not doing justice to some of her favorite dishes. She suggested several tricks, and the next day she suggested a few more. Soon it became clear to all that Zimam was more than a dishwasher. She was promoted, and very quickly began to manage the whole kitchen. For four and a half years, she ran the kitchen while she worked a second job. Then she bought the restaurant. Cafe Eritrea has been a focal point for Eritrean culture in the area ever since. Whether Zimam is catering a wedding for 100, or feeding a sole Eritrean traveler looking for some taste of home, the dimly lit restaurant offers the tastes and flavors so many people in the area yearn for.

From standing at her mother's waist watching her cut vegetables, to stirring a pot of onions and garlic so large it could feed 100 people, and probably will, Zimam has always found herself a home through food. So, if you are strolling through the neighborhood, look out for the red banner and the big buffet sign. Say hello to the patron at the bar, find yourself a seat, and prepare for a delicious home-cooked meal.

The Eritrean meal is almost always a shared one. Injera, a fermented and spongy flatbread, is laid on a big platter and all the foods that are being eaten are placed around the perimeter of the plate on top of the bread...

KULWA

Yields 3-4 portions

Freshly made Injera bread is available at Cafe Eritrea D'Afrique (Oakland).

Corrorima ("false cardamom") and Berber chili powder are available at Ras Dashen Market (Oakland).

Chili Paste

1 red onion, chopped roughly

4 cloves garlic, peeled

2 tablespoons Berber chili powder

¾ teaspoon salt

Beef

Olive oil, for pan frying

1 ½ large Roma tomatoes, chopped roughly

¼ onion, chopped roughly

2 cloves garlic, chopped finely

5 tablespoons chili paste (from above)

1 teaspoon ghee

½ teaspoon ground corrorima

½ teaspoon ground cumin

¼ teaspoon salt

¾ pound top sirloin beef, cut in ⅓ inch cubes

2 tablespoons Ayib cheese or Greek yogurt

DIRECTIONS

For the paste

Yields about 1 cup

Blend the onion, garlic, Berber chili powder, and salt in a food processor or blender until no chunks of onion or garlic remain. Set aside.

For the beef

Heat a high-sided pan over high heat, and add enough olive oil to coat the bottom. Add the tomato and onion and cook until the tomatoes begin to stick to the bottom of the pan and all the juices have cooked off (5-6 minutes). Turn the heat to medium and add the garlic and chili paste along with one tablespoon of water. Add the ghee, corrorima, cumin, and salt.

Add the sirloin to the pan and cook until a piece of beef sliced in half is slightly pink and tender (6-8 minutes).

Top with Ayib or yogurt to finish.

HAMLI

Yields 3-4 portions

1 bunch collard greens, rinsed

1 Roma tomato, chopped roughly

¼ onion, chopped roughly

4–5 cloves garlic, chopped finely

¼ teaspoon salt

½ teaspoon ground black pepper

½ teaspoon cumin

1 small jalapeño, seeded and chopped finely

DIRECTIONS

Slice the collard greens widthwise in ⅓ inch strips.

Heat a medium pot over medium high heat. When a piece of tomato placed in the pan sizzles, add the tomato and onion and sauté until they begin to break down and liquid is released from the tomatoes (2–3 minutes). It is okay if the tomatoes stick to the pan. Add the garlic and continue to cook the mixture down on high heat for one minute.

Turn the heat to medium low and add the collard greens, salt, black pepper, and cumin. Allow the collard greens to wilt and cook down (4–5 minutes).

Remove the pot from the heat and add the chopped jalapeño.

Enjoy with Kulwa over injera.

55

PORK POTSTICKERS

OAK CENTER, OAKLAND   JACKIE

This recipe calls for a homemade dumpling dough. You could, of course, substitute a store-bought alternative, but I strongly recommend that you don't. Not only is the dough forgiving, but after you make this recipe, you will most likely have left-over dumplings. Freeze them in bags and you will be very happy to run across them some time when you're looking for berries or ice cream. You can tackle the forming of these dumplings on your own, or you can call in a few friends to join in the fun. The first few dumplings you make might not look like the photographs, but they will get much better as you go along

WHEN WE REACHED JACKIE'S HOUSE, in the Oak Center neighborhood of West Oakland, only a few minutes from Chinatown, she was midway through boxing up and organizing supplies for her small beer-brewing operation. With brightly dyed hair and an air that lets you know she means business, you probably want to end up on her good side. As soon as she begins to speak, however, it becomes clear that she is among the sweetest people you will ever meet.

Jackie grew up in San Leandro. Her mother came directly from China, and her father is third generation Chinese American, born and raised in Oakland. Out her back window, we could see the very tops of Jackie's tomato plants. The whole garden was, in fact, filled with tomatoes, alongside a small patch of garlic chives. A bundle of fresh-picked chives rested on the counter.

Surrounded by the stainless steel and cast iron pots and pans that hung from hooks on the walls, Jackie began to pound out and mix the ground pork she had just gotten at New Hop Lung Meat Market, her favorite butcher shop in Chinatown, where the meat is ground fresh on request. We were set to make Potstickers. Jackie explained that

Jackie explained that cooking was relatively new to her, something that was hard to believe as she effortlessly rolled out and began to fill the potsticker dough she had made…

cooking was relatively new to her, something that was hard to believe as she effortlessly rolled out and began to fill the potsticker dough she had made.

Jackie had not cooked at all before meeting her husband, seven years ago. He is from Germany, near the French border, and when Jackie met his family, she started to watch and learn to make some of the German classics—Spaetzel, Potato Salad, the works. Until she met her husband, Jackie would often head back to her parents' house around dinner time to pick up a plate of food and check in. As she learned to make dishes from her husband's family and looked back on her childhood, so full of delicious foods, Jackie began to cook more and more often.

By no means was Jackie lacking exposure to good food when she was growing up. Her grandmother did a vast amount of the cooking at home, and the whole extended family would come together often to enjoy each other's company around a table laden with Potstickers, Sweet and Sticky Barbecued Pork, eggplant (which Jackie would not touch) and anything else which had caught her grandmother's eye at the market that day. Jackie remembers the mostly wonderful flavors and smells of her childhood: Durian, known by some as the world's stinkiest fruit; and ginger, which usually headed into the pot to make an Egg Ginger Soup served to friends who were pregnant; or maybe the crab that the family ate on Thanksgiving instead of turkey.

Her grandmother also tended the garden, something else Jackie has only recently found her love for—although she cited this as having something to do, in the past, with being unable to keep anything alive.

If Jackie is not working, cooking, or tending to her tomato plants, she and her husband head over to B-Dama, a Japanese restaurant located in Swan's Marketplace in

Old Oakland. For lunch, Vietnamese sandwiches from Cam Huong in Chinatown are often on the menu. And if stomachs are still rumbling, they will head over to Abura-Ya, a fried chicken spot she described as "punkish" in style. And though she doesn't succumb to the craving as often, when she was little, the Mexican Bun at Ruby King Bakery Cafe was a real treat.

Jackie spends as much time as she can at the Mountain View Cemetery, where her grandparents are buried. On a clear day, she visits their graves and sits and watches over the entire San Francisco Bay, while turkeys run wild around her.

Jackie has turned from the child who could not keep her plants alive and who rarely strayed into the kitchen, into a cook, a gardener, and a brewer. When you make these dumplings, you will understand the love that goes into each step, gently pleating, frying, and eating the delectable morsels.

PORK POTSTICKERS

Yields 80-100 potstickers

Extra potstickers can be frozen and cooked later

Dough

3 cups + scant ½ cup all purpose flour + more for dusting

1 cup warm water

1 ½ tablespoons salt

Filling

½ medium Napa cabbage

1 teaspoon salt

2 pounds pork shoulder, ground

2 tablespoons olive oil

2 tablespoons light soy sauce

1 tablespoon rice wine

1 ½ teaspoons sesame oil

5 tablespoons gelatinous bone stock or water

1 bunch green onions, peeled and chopped into thin rounds

1 bunch garlic chives, chopped finely

Vegetable oil, for pan frying

Dipping Sauce

¼ cup white vinegar

¼ cup light soy sauce

DIRECTIONS

For the dough

In a medium bowl combine the flour, water, and salt. Knead lightly to combine. The dough will be flaky at this point. Pour the dough onto a clean, floured countertop and knead until very smooth and workable (8–10 minutes). The dough should be firm. If it is so hard it is unworkable, sprinkle it with ½ teaspoon water and knead for another 2–3 minutes.

Wrap tightly in plastic wrap and rest at room temperature for 30 minutes, or for up to 12 hours in the refrigerator. On your floured surface, form the dough into a ball and divide into 4 equally sized pieces. Roll each piece into a 1 inch thick log. Cut each log into ¾ inch thick rounds. Roll out each round, turning as you roll to form a circle about ⅙ inch thick and 3–4 inches in diameter.

For the filling

Finely slice the cabbage and place it in a medium bowl. Add the salt. Squeeze and work the cabbage vigorously to draw out the water. Drain and repeat once more.

Add the pork, olive oil, light soy sauce, rice wine, sesame oil, bone stock, green onions and garlic chives to the drained cabbage in a medium bowl. Fry off a small patty of the mixture on the stovetop to taste for seasoning. Balance the seasoning and fry off one more small patty, until you are satisfied with the flavor. Using a wooden spatula or your hands, work the ground pork mixture until it is pasty and smooth.

Cover the wrappers with a damp towel while you form individual potstickers. Add 1 ½ tablespoons of the pork filling to the center of a wrapper. Fold the wrapper in half, pinching the two sides together

where they meet in the middle. Starting from one side of the potsticker, fold and pleat until you reach the middle, pressing hard to ensure both sides are well sealed. Repeat the pleating process from the other side so the potsticker is securely closed.

Heat a large cast iron pan over medium high heat, and add enough vegetable oil to coat the bottom. Place as many potstickers in the pan as you can without them touching. Fry until the bottoms are golden brown and crisp.

Pour enough water into the pan to cover the bottom (¼–⅓ cup) and cover the pan until the water has cooked off (2-3 minutes).

Remove one potsticker from the pan, and check that the pork is no longer pink and is fully cooked. If the potstickers are not fully cooked, add another ¼ cup water and cover the pan to finish.

Continue to cook the potstickers in batches.

Arrange on a large platter and serve with dipping sauce.

CHILLED RED BEET SOUP

MONTCLAIR, OAKLAND   LENA

After you make this refreshing soup once, you will want it every time the sun begins to burn hot and high in the sky. When you are looking for something light, the base recipe will be perfect. Add a little more sour cream and an extra egg, and you have a more substantial dish. Do as you see fit, adding chopped tarragon or other delicious fresh herbs from your garden.

LENA'S FAMILY LIVES in the beautiful hills of Montclair, nestled into the trees. Sun shines in through her kitchen window and illuminates the bright marble countertops. Freshly gathered eggs from her chicken coop lie on a ceramic platter on the dining room table. The shelves and bookcases of Lena's home are adorned with matryoshka nesting dolls and souvenirs from her family's trips back to her native Russia.

When Lena was a child, cooking always took place with several other people in the kitchen, laughing and putting a meal together for the family. Growing up in a culture where cooking was a shared activity, it did not become apparent to Lena how laborious Russian cooking could be until she moved away from her family. In America, she cooked Russian food alone. That was when she realized how much precise work went into putting a traditional meal together. "All my friends want to make borscht until they realize how many steps it takes," Lena told us.

The soup provided
perfect relief on a day
when all we wanted
to do was find a shady
patch of grass around
Lake Merritt and take
a nap…

Lena decided she would teach us to make a dish that is popular in Russia during the summer—a cold beet soup. We began to understand what Lena meant about the meticulous nature of Russian cooking as we watched her carefully divide and chop the cucumbers, beets, and eggs. The soup provided perfect relief on a day when all we wanted to do was find a shady patch of grass around Lake Merritt and take a nap.

Lena grew up in Ivanovo, a city in Southern Russia near the Black Sea. She learned to cook from her mother and her grandmothers. Every day, when her mother got home from work, she would put a pan on the stove and ask Lena, "What are we going to cook today?" Food was a surefire way to connect with family. Every meal felt like Thanksgiving. In preparation for winter, Lena and her mother canned fruits and vegetables and put on large pots of borscht to keep the whole family warm and content.

As a child, Lena imagined she would always live in the town with her mother, siblings, and grandparents. She might have, but when she was in her last year of college, Mark came to give a lecture and they fell in love. Mark's job moved them to the Bay Area, where they unpacked their bags and started a new life together.

Lena makes sure her three daughters do not lose touch with the culture she loves so much. Every year the family takes a long trip back to Russia. While the family is there, her daughters do all the same things as everyone else in town—sweeping the house, cleaning dishes, and cooking meals. In the morning, the girls bring baskets to the small vendors' market and pick up fresh eggs, still-warm milk, and steaming hot bread.

Oakland has a strong Russian community, and Lena is able to find many of the foods here that she loved to eat in Ivanovo: Big baskets of herring, without the salty brine, are easily available at Euromix, a European delicatessen on Piedmont Avenue.

When Lena has guests over for dinner, she is still surprised they do not expect her to make more than a salad and one main dish. "When you go to a Russian restaurant, you order a bunch of things until you can't see the tablecloth." Her mother faced an unfortunate surprise when she visited from Russia and tried to do the same thing at an American restaurant. Not realizing how large American portions were, she was bombarded with more food than she knew what to do with.

Lena is often in her kitchen making dinner, just as she once did with her mother. On arriving home from school, Lena's daughters are met by the exciting smells and rituals of Lena's childhood. Now, every day when her daughters get home from school, Lena can ask them, "What are we going to cook today?"

CHILLED BEET SOUP

Yields 6–8 portions as a first course

3 medium red beets, peeled

3 eggs, hard-boiled

2 Persian or pickling cucumbers

Salt

1 green onion, peeled and chopped into thin rounds

Sour cream

White vinegar

DIRECTIONS

In a medium pot, boil enough water to cover the beets. Boil the beets until they can easily be pierced with a knife (30–40 minutes). Remove beets from the pot and chill the beet broth (1–3 hours).

Peel the hard-boiled eggs. Sometimes it is easiest to crack the egg shells gently on a hard surface and peel the eggs immersed in a bowl of cold water.

Slice the eggs, beets, and cucumbers into small pieces (roughly ⅛ inch cubes).

Assembly

Mix the finely chopped beets, eggs, and cucumbers in a small bowl and salt to taste. Put a generous helping (about ¾ cup) of the egg mixture into each soup bowl. Ladle a serving (about ¾ cup) of the chilled beet broth into each bowl.

Garnish with green onion, a dollop of sour cream, and a dash of white vinegar. The vinegar and sour cream can be left on the table for guests to balance the soup as they like.

MA PO TOFU & HOT AND SOUR SOUP

TEMESCAL, OAKLAND   CHUNG

Hot and Sour Soup and Ma Po Tofu are both simple, comforting, and extremely delicious. The soup is similar to one you would get at a really good Chinese restaurant. Chung recommends strongly that you adjust all the flavors so it is exactly the way you like. If spice is what you are looking for, add a little more white pepper; if milder, then less. The Ma Po Tofu should also be adjusted to your taste and can very easily be made in big batches if you want to have friends over.

CHUNG LIVES IN THE TEMESCAL neighborhood of Oakland, and decided he would rather come to us to cook. When the doorbell rang, there stood a compact and smiling man. In his arms, he held a large cardboard box full of the ingredients he was pretty sure our fridge did not contain. He was correct. Chung was followed in the door by his daughter, there to help translate some of his longer thoughts and instructions from Mandarin to English.

Chung was full of energy. He told us that he had worked in restaurants for 30 years, but was retired now. It was hard to imagine him lying around the house or basking in the sun for longer then a few minutes.

He hails from Jiayi, Taiwan but he moved to Taipei when he was eight, and it was in Taipei that he grew up. The city was overflowing with the food from all the regions of China, brought by the people who had fled to Taiwan in search of freedom and safety. A young Chung enjoyed the cooking of his mother, the mild and sweet foods typical of the Zhejiang province where she had lived. As a child, he recalls feasting on

many of his favorite foods: Xiao Long Bao—traditional soup dumplings that explode with hot flavorful soup when punctured, crispy potstickers, steamed rice, and Ma Po Tofu and Hot and Sour Soup. As he was talking about his childhood, Chung delicately sliced green onions into long thin rounds to sprinkle over the soup. He looked up, smiling. "More beautiful like this."

Chung did not grow up cooking, but he certainly made up for it when he reached America. As he pulled canned bamboo shoots and little jars of garlic bean paste and sesame oil out of his heaping box, Chung told us about his decision to come to America. When he was 28 he got on a plane headed for San Francisco. He had friends in the States but his family all stayed in Taiwan.

San Francisco did not feel too different from Tapei to Chung. Nearly as soon as his plane landed, he began to work in restaurants. He learned quickly and only spent three years at the first restaurant in San Francisco before opening his own restaurant in Hayward. Eventually, the restaurant moved to Piedmont Avenue in Oakland, and then from there to College Avenue.

While we were talking, Chung abruptly stood and walked out onto the back porch for a breath of fresh air. As Chung cooled off and bounced on the heels of his feet, his daughter reminisced about growing up in his restaurants, running through the kitchen, learning a few words of Spanish from the man washing dishes, and eating most of her meals there. Then Chung was back in the kitchen, wielding pots and pans as we worked hard to keep up—flashing photos here and there and frantically writing down his tips and advice.

If Chung is not in his kitchen cooking the foods he loves to make, he may be at Peony Seafood Restaurant in Chinatown, enjoying tea and dining on Siu Mai, stuffed with ground pork or shrimp, Barbecue Pork Buns, full of sweet and succulent pork pieces, and maybe some of the chicken feet which are largely passed up by tourists coming through the area.

Since his daughter was old enough to travel, the family has been going back to Taiwan every year, where Chung learns to cook new things. Sadly, you won't be able to eat at his restaurant anymore, but that does not mean you can't enjoy at least two of the dishes he was so proud to serve. Next time you decide to make a new dish or enjoy an old one, do as Chung has done for so long, and make it beautiful.

Chung delicately sliced green onions into long thin rounds to sprinkle over the soup. He looked up, smiling. "More beautiful like this…"

MA PO TOFU

Yields 4-6 portions

Szechuan chili bean pastes are available in great variety at Berkeley Bowl (Berkeley) and 99 Ranch Market (Richmond).

2 (16 ounce) containers silken tofu

Olive oil, for pan frying

2 cloves garlic, sliced thinly

1 inch ginger, peeled, smashed with side of knife, chopped finely

1 green onion, peeled and chopped into thin rounds

½ pound ground pork

2 ½ teaspoons Szechuan chili bean paste

⅓ cup chicken stock

1 ½ tablespoons oyster sauce

2 tablespoons light soy sauce

White pepper

2 tablespoons cornstarch, dissolved in 2 tablespoons water

⅛ teaspoon sesame oil

DIRECTIONS

Cut tofu in 1 inch cubes. Heat a large cast iron pan over medium heat, and add enough olive oil to coat the bottom.

Add garlic, ginger, ½ of the green onion, and the pork to the pan. When the pork is lightly browned (3-5 minutes), incorporate the chili paste.

Add the chicken stock and tofu to the pan along with the oyster sauce, soy sauce, and a dash of white pepper.

Turn heat to high and add the cornstarch mixture slowly, stirring until the liquid in the pan has thickened noticeably.

Remove from the heat, taste for seasoning, and finish with several drops of sesame oil and the remaining green onion.

HOT AND SOUR SOUP

Yields 6–8 portions

2 quarts (8 cups) chicken stock

1 tablespoon white pepper

1 (4–6 ounce) chicken breast, cut in 1 to 2 inch cubes

1 (14 ounce) package medium-firm tofu, cut in 1 ½ inch long, ¼ inch thick strips

⅔ cup light soy sauce

⅓ cup + extra white vinegar

2 green onions, peeled and chopped into thin rounds

½ cup cornstarch, dissolved in ½ cup water

4 eggs, whisked

6 dried wood-ear or shiitake mushrooms, reconstituted in warm water and chopped in ⅓ inch wide strips

1 (19 ounce) can halved bamboo shoots, drained and chopped in 1 ½ inch long, ¼ inch thick strips (same size as tofu)

DIRECTIONS

In a medium pot bring the chicken stock to a gentle boil. Add the chicken and white pepper, and cook until the chicken begins to turn white (2-3 minutes). Add the tofu, soy sauce, vinegar, and half of the chopped green onions.

Taste, making sure the acidity and spice are balanced to your liking. Adjust by adding more white pepper or vinegar. Add the cornstarch mixture and stir to incorporate.

Turn to medium low and very slowly pour in the eggs while stirring constantly. They will 'flower' in the soup and form long strands. Add the mushrooms and bamboo shoots.

Finish in bowls with the remaining green onion.

QUICK GRILLED RIBS

REDWOOD HEIGHTS, OAKLAND   YULANDA

In an era of forty-eight hour marinades and three-day braises, these ribs are an amazing exception—you can eat them today. Yulanda has created a perfectly penetrating mixture of sweet, spicy, and salty that doesn't require a single moment of marination. As soon as the coals heat up, dinner is on the way.

ON SUNNY DAYS in the Redwood Heights neighborhood of Oakland, if Yulanda does not have a catering gig, you will find her with a group of friends standing by her grill in the backyard as the tantalizing aromas of black pepper and paprika fill the hot air above the coals. With a bright smile and a loud, boisterous laugh, you cannot miss her.

Yulanda grew up in Benton Harbor, Michigan, in the southwest corner of the state. The school year was spent in Michigan, but the summers were spent at her grandmother's hog farm in Tennessee. Winter or summer, she was always around cooks and good food. Yulanda's mother was a chef, trained in Italian cooking. Adding a Southern twist, her mother would make lots of fried chicken, but also homemade fettuccine—always fettuccine, because the family did not own a pasta machine and the pizza cutter made only long, straight pasta.

Yulanda learned from her mother to be smart and careful with her ingredients. As Yulanda sprinkled her homemade seasoning mix over the raw ribs, she told us that despite having worked with countless "master chefs" over the years, her mother, aunt, and grandma were three of the best chefs she has ever known.

From working for a multi-million-dollar catering empire, she went to wheeling her $10 grill to sporting events...

After going to college and deciding she did not want to be an engineer, she moved with her girlfriend to Chicago. They spent several months getting to know the city, while Yulanda waited out her residency requirement so she could attend an accredited culinary program at the community college. When school ended, her professor offered her an opportunity she could not resist: a job working as a chef at a resort in Jamaica.

In her six months at the resort, Yulanda faced a harsh reality: women in the kitchens were only allowed to work the salad station or make pastries. The higher profile cooking was all done by men.

On her return to Chicago, Yulanda got a job working for Wolfgang Puck, helping to create the Wolfgang Puck packaged food line. She worked for his brand for six years, doing events for as many as 600 people at a time. She was climbing her way up the ranks, and expected to be the next executive chef at one of his restaurants. Yulanda was training her new sous chef just as Wolfgang opened a new restaurant. When they sent the sous chef, a young white man, to fill the new spot as executive chef, it was the "straw that broke the camel's back."

She walked away from Wolfgang Puck and never looked back. Her girlfriend at the time convinced her to open a small catering company. From working for a multi-million dollar food empire, she went to wheeling her $10 grill to sporting events. One of the last events Yulanda worked after splitting up with her girlfriend was the Michigan Music Festival. There, she met Lisa, now her long-time partner.

Today, Yulanda owns a catering company called Simply Bliss. With the fresh ingredients that are so readily available in the Oakland area, Yulanda has become known for her flexible and innovative menus. She is skilled at accommodating whatever dietary restrictions her clients send her way, and she has always been ahead of the curve. The new idea of "farm to table" seems funny to Yulanda. She laughed as she told us that when she was growing up, it wasn't a choice—you just cooked that way because the cheapest way to eat was from your farm to your table!

When it is too rainy for the Weber grill to light up, and there are no weddings to be catered, the family eats dinner in a cool corner of Ensarro, one of Oakland's beloved Ethiopian restaurants.

In the urban environment that is the Redwood Heights neighborhood, there are no hog farms in sight and the nearest open reaches of green harvest fields are hours away, but you would not be able to tell by the way Yulanda cooks. Her kitchen is wherever she chooses to set up, whether under a tent in the church parking lot, in her well-equipped home, or on the grill in the backyard.

There has never been a moment of doubt in her mind that she made the right decision saying goodbye to Wolfgang Puck and rolling out the grill. The care Yulanda puts into her food is clear. Maybe she was inspired by her mom's use-everything style of cooking, or maybe it was Wolfgang Puck's high cuisine that developed her palate. Whatever it was, we are lucky to have Yulanda in Oakland.

QUICK GRILLED RIBS

Yields 4-6 portions

1 rack (2 ½ – 3 pounds) Saint Louis style ribs, back flap removed

1 ½ tablespoons salt

1 tablespoon black pepper

2 teaspoons onion powder

2 teaspoons paprika

1 tablespoon garlic powder

1 teaspoon cumin

Barbecue sauce, optional

DIRECTIONS

Set up a coal fire and when the coals are red-hot, spread them evenly.

While the grate is heating, slice through the thin membrane in between each rib parallel to the bone. This will make the ribs easy to cut and serve when they are finished. Combine the spices and rub both sides of the ribs with the seasoning mixture.

Put the seasoned ribs on the grill, presentation side down. Let the ribs brown and caramelize on both sides (5-6 minutes each side).

Remove ribs from the grill and cut the rack into quarters. Tightly wrap each segment with aluminum foil.

Move the coals to one side of the grill and put the rib packages back on the grill over indirect heat. Cover the grill with the vent cracked open and cook for 30 to 35 minutes before removing to a platter.

Brush the ribs with your favorite BBQ sauce. Let them rest several minutes before serving.

PHYLLO-WRAPPED CHICKEN BREAST

PIEDMONT PINES, OAKLAND   LIANE

This is about as close to a one-pot meal as you can get without the pot. Folding and wrapping each chicken parcel in flaky, buttery phyllo dough is meditative and relaxing at the end of a long day, while not taking very long or requiring much clean-up. The chicken is moist and perfectly cooked every time, the phyllo dough crispy and chewy in all the right places. Freeze the half box of phyllo you do not use; it will come in handy again next time you want to bake a pan of these delicious little parcels.

LIANE'S HOUSE SITS atop a hill in the Piedmont Pines neighborhood. As she cleared off her kitchen counter, Liane explained to us that the dish she was making was most delicious with fresh phyllo—a light flaky pastry dough she can no longer find in stores. Liane is an avid cook, organizing her friends to make dinners together, and writing her own recipes. Phyllo-Wrapped Chicken Breast with Orange and Avocado Salsa is one of the many dishes she loves to make.

Liane grew up with her grandmother, her parents, and a younger sister. When her parents were young, they both experienced the harsh reality of discrimination in America. Her mother was put in an internment camp during World War II and her father was kicked out of Stanford because of his Japanese roots, despite being an American citizen. When the war was over, and life was returning to some form of normality, they did what many Japanese immigrants did, and decided the best way to raise their children was not to teach them Japanese, and to encourage them

An hour outside of
Fukuoka, Liane found
an entire branch of her
family she had never
known about...

to assimilate as quickly as possible. It was hard for Liane to communicate with her Japanese-born grandmother. Without speaking more than a few words of English, her grandmother would stand in the kitchen cooking classic American dishes—meat and potatoes. Her mother and grandmother were both fabulous cooks. Liane grew up eating lots of dishes from other parts of the world, but few from Japan.

When Liane left for college, she realized she needed to start cooking if she was going to keep eating the foods she had loved so much growing up. She went to UC Berkeley, and began to take cooking classes while she worked her way through school. She met her husband at Berkeley, and they married as soon as they graduated.

When Liane's husband finished school, they began to house-hunt. After eight months of searching with no success, they finally found the house where they have now lived for 40 years. The house is tall and beautiful, pushed far up against a hill. A garden in the back scales the hill and is full of bright flowers and draping vines.

It was not until Liane had children that she began to reconnect with her Japanese roots. The kids were interested in their heritage and Liane's daughter loved her fifth grade teacher, who had taught English in Japan. He was involved with Sister Cities International, a nonprofit organization that aims to connect cities from different sides of the world through friendship and diplomacy. Oakland's Japanese sister city is Fukuoka.

Her children's interest in their culture gave Liane a second chance to connect with her heritage. The relationship between Oakland and its sister city inspired the family to go to Japan. An hour outside of Fukuoka, Liane found an entire branch of her family she had never known about.

Since Liane first visited Japan, she has gone back on many occasions. But Oakland always remains home. In the years she has lived in Oakland, the city has changed dramatically. When BART built a train line going through downtown, the streets were torn up to put in the stations. Liane and her husband speculate that this is the reason downtown struggled for so long. They have only recently started to notice an increase in business, although retail businesses still have not made a full return.

On most days, Liane is in her hilly backyard garden, pruning and tending to the plants that attract so many bees and birds. When she is not in her garden, you may find her and her husband dining at Iyasare, a Japanese restaurant on 4th street in Berkeley, or Wood Tavern, an American restaurant on College Avenue in Oakland that focuses on fresh local ingredients and fine wines.

Throughout Liane's deepening relationship with her culture, she has continued to learn about other people's traditions and absorb new recipes. Liane makes traditional Japanese foods more often now, but she is just as likely to be cooking spinach noodles with a meat sauce for her favorite green lasagna or carefully folding chicken in sheets of phyllo.

PHYLLO-WRAPPED CHICKEN BREAST

Yields 8 portions

The phyllo should be defrosted in the refrigerator for 8-12 hours.

Chicken

1 cup mayonnaise

1 green onion, peeled and chopped into thin rounds

2 tablespoons lemon juice

½ teaspoon fresh thyme leaves

6 cloves garlic, chopped finely

¾ cup finely grated Parmigiano Reggiano cheese + more for finishing

1 stick (4 ounces) butter

½ cup vegetable oil

4 (⅓-½ pound) boneless skinless chicken breasts, cut in half widthwise

8 sheets phyllo dough (½ of a 1 pound package)

Salt and pepper

Orange Avocado Salsa

2 large oranges, Cara Cara are ideal

2 large avocados

½ red onion, chopped finely

1-2 tablespoons rice wine vinegar

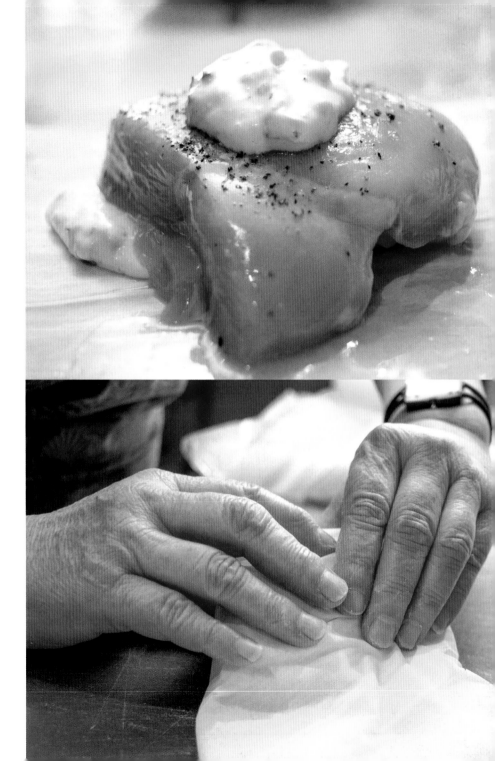

DIRECTIONS

Preheat the oven to 375 degrees.

For the chicken

Combine the mayonnaise, green onion, lemon juice, thyme, ⅔ of the garlic, and ¼ cup of the parmesan.

In a small pot, melt the butter over medium heat. Remove from heat, add the vegetable oil and the remaining garlic, and set aside.

Blot the chicken dry with a paper towel.

Cut the phyllo sheets in half width-wise to make 16 half-sized sheets of dough.

While you work, make sure to keep the phyllo sheets covered with a lightly dampened towel. Otherwise, the dough dries out and becomes fragile and brittle.

Lay two half-sheets of phyllo dough on a cutting board, stacked on top of each other, and gently brush with a light layer of the butter garlic mixture. Place a teaspoon of the mayonnaise mixture on one of the corners of the sheet. Place one of the halved chicken breasts on top of the mayonnaise and top with one more teaspoon of the mayonnaise mixture. Sprinkle lightly with salt and pepper.

To form each package, fold the chicken and phyllo on a diagonal to form a triangle. Butter each layer as you fold. Fold again to seal the triangle and fold any excess phyllo over to complete the package. Slice away any remaining dough.

Place the phyllo packets on an un-greased baking sheet and paint the top of each packet with butter. Sprinkle the remaining parmesan over the tops of each packet. Bake in the preheated oven for 25–30 minutes, until phyllo is lightly browned and crisp.

For the salsa

Peel, segment, and chop the oranges into small bite-size pieces. Cut the avocados to the same size as the oranges. Mix the oranges, avocados, red onion, and 1 tablespoon of the vinegar. Taste for acidity and add the second tablespoon of vinegar if necessary.

Place a phyllo parcel on the center of each plate with a generous side of salsa.

REINA PEPIADA AREPAS

NEWTOWN, OAKLAND   MILENA

The allure of the arepa may have something to do with the crisp, warm patty that can be filled with nearly anything, or it could be the hefty slice of cool butter with which you are encouraged to adorn the arepa. Although the recipe offers a measurement for water, you might make these without a measuring cup after you get comfortable. Depending on who you eat these with, the customs are very different. Some people like to scrape out the chewy center to make more room for filling; others find the chewy inside their favorite part. You will quickly begin to understand why generations of Venezuelans have relied on endless variations of this dish to fill their breakfast, lunch and dinner plates.

MILENA LIVES IN WEST OAKLAND. This may not be the first place you would expect to find Victorian houses and tall trees, but that is just one of the surprises awaiting you in the Newtown neighborhood. Tall graceful peaks and bright colors give this house the picture perfect feel that, as it turns out, is typical of many houses in this part of the city.

Milena is from Caracas, Venezuela's largest city. Caracas is in the north, a vibrant city jam-packed with people, surrounded by hills, and very near the Caribbean Sea. Milena grew up with her mother, father, and sister. Her grandparents would come and stay months on end with the family. In Caracas, Milena never had to worry when playing outside. She would hang out on the streets playing games with her friends until she was called in for lunch or dinner.

When she was 16, Milena decided she wanted to be a vegetarian. Around the same time, her father was told by a doctor that his diet needed to improve, and suddenly vegetarianism became a family project. When the house was emptied of all meat

These areperias are the number one destination for many schoolchildren after a long day of classes, and stay open until the crack of dawn to satisfy the rumbling stomachs of late night patrons and party-goers...

products, aunt and grandma had no choice but to reluctantly transition to a meat-free way of eating and cooking. Milena's grandma switched out chicken for soy protein in her empanadas. It was at this point that Milena and her sister began baking their own breads, making yogurt, and exploring the new food world they had found. Although Milena is not a vegetarian anymore, she looks back fondly on the years that sparked her interest in food.

We stood in Milena's beautiful, high-ceilinged kitchen while she formed an arepa dough. Arepas are corn patties cooked on a scaldingly hot cast iron pan and then baked in a hot oven until they puff and fill with steam. The arepas are sliced open, coated with butter and filled with various delicious fillings. In Caracas, you would be hard-pressed to find a corner that was not home to an areperia. These areperias are the number one destination for many school-children after a long day of classes, and they stay open until the crack of dawn to satisfy the rumbling stomachs of late night patrons and party-goers.

When Milena was 20, she left Venezuela and came to America. She ended up in San Francisco, a city where she had always wanted to live. There, she met her husband at a party. While living in San Francisco, Milena regularly came to the East Bay to visit friends. Originally, she much preferred visiting Berkeley, where it seemed safer. It was certainly quieter. When her husband got a job in Oakland, he found them a beautiful house in a neighborhood where Milena hadn't expected to end up.

Oakland did not have the reassuring safety she had been so comfortable with in Venezuela. Since she got here ten years ago, the city has not stopped changing. Over time, she has come to love her neighborhood and the community of friends she has formed. It is starting to feel like the city Milena has always hoped for.

In Venezuelan culture, like so many others, family meals are an important and never-missed part of daily life. In Milena's home, breakfast is a routine family gathering. Before everyone rushes off for school and work, they sit together for a meal, usually consisting of arepas stuffed with beans and cheese.

Almost 4000 miles from her original home, Milena brings together the fragrant and comforting flavors of her childhood. With a burst of steam and melted butter, happy memories flood back. It may be hard to find an areperia in Oakland, so when it starts to get cold out or you get home late and crave something simple and comforting, crank on that oven, pull out your corn flour, and get started.

REINA PEPIADA AREPAS

Yields 14 arepas

Harina P.A.N. is available at Mi Tierra Foods (Berkeley)

Chicken salad

2 (10 ounce) boneless skinless chicken breasts

2 avocados

1 tablespoon white vinegar

¼ cup mayonnaise

¼ bunch cilantro, stemmed, chopped finely

¼ bunch flat leaf parsley, stemmed, chopped finely

½ red bell pepper, chopped finely

½ red onion, chopped finely

1 green onion, peeled and chopped into thin rounds

½ jalapeño, seeded and chopped finely

Poaching

4 garlic cloves, crushed

1 medium onion, chopped roughly

1 ½ teaspoons salt

1 teaspoon crushed black pepper

Arepa dough

4 cups Harina P.A.N. white corn flour

1 tablespoon salt

4 cups warm water

Olive oil, for pan frying

DIRECTIONS

For poaching the chicken

In a medium pot over high heat, boil enough water to cover the chicken breasts. Add the garlic, onion, salt, and pepper. Cook the chicken until two forks can easily pull the meat apart (15-20 minutes). Strain chicken and set aside to let cool.

For the chicken salad

Scoop the avocados into a medium bowl and smash with a fork until there are no large chunks remaining. Add white vinegar and mayonnaise along with the cilantro, parsley, bell pepper, red onion, and green onion. Add jalapeño to taste, depending on spice preference. Start with ½ jalapeño and add accordingly.

Shred the cooled chicken and add to the avocado mixture.

Taste for salt and pepper.

Cover and refrigerate if you do not plan to start the dough immediately.

For the arepa dough

Preheat the oven to 375 degrees.

In a medium bowl mix the salt and Harina P.A.N. Slowly mix the warm water into the Harina P.A.N. The dough should be smooth and workable, and should not crack on the edges when you form the patties. Continue to pour the water and stir with your hands until the dough is soft and smooth. Knead the dough until all bubbles of flour are gone and the dough is very smooth and workable. Rest the dough for 10 minutes.

Heat a large cast iron pan over medium-high heat. Segment the dough into 14 pieces and roll each into a ball about 2 inches in diameter. Push the dough balls down into discs about ¼ inch thick and 4½ inches wide.

Rub down the cast iron pan with an olive oil-dampened paper towel. Fry patties until their bottoms have become crisp and golden brown, and no longer stick to the pan (2-3 minutes). Flip and cook until both sides are crisp and the patties begin to sound hollow when tapped. Patties can go directly from the pan onto the racks in the oven or onto a baking sheet. When the patties begin to puff slightly in the oven, they are done (10-12 minutes).

Remove patties to a basket and cover with a cloth towel to contain the heat.

Assembly

Make a slice in the edge of a patty, opening the arepa and creating a pocket you can fill. The insides of the arepas are soft and you can scrape away some of the insides to make more space for filling. Some people think the chewy insides are the best part. You decide.

Place a thin slice of butter in the steaming hot center of the patty. Fill with a heaping serving of chicken salad and serve with hot sauce.

RICOTTA GNOCCHI

PIEDMONT AVENUE, OAKLAND   NICK

If you have ever made traditional potato gnocchi, this ricotta-filled alternative may seem like a surprising version. All the movements are gentle—from stirring the cheeses to forming the dumplings, you will not knead or pound once. You end up adding a lot of personality to a recipe like this, because it is unlikely to come out exactly the same twice in a row, regardless of what you do. Depending on the moisture of the ricotta, or the dryness of the parmesan, little variables make these dumplings taste slightly different every time.

NICK'S HOUSE LIES at the end of a quiet and peaceful road branching off of Piedmont Avenue. Nick opens the door, a tall guy sporting a button-up shirt peppered with Mexican wrestling masks, cacti, and tropical cocktails. In a shoutout to his Italian heritage, Nick is going to be making ricotta gnocchi—much lighter and less chewy fare than its potato-based cousin. The smell of fresh sage and toasting butter welcomes us in.

When Nick was a young child, the kitchen was a mysterious and awe-inspiring place, and a place where people congregated—whether it was his father throwing together elaborate recipes from unusual ingredients, a style of cooking he learned as he worked his way through San Francisco in the 70's and 80's, or his mother's more classical American style of cooking, which she got from her upbringing on a small ranch outside of Stockton, California.

Nick's first cooking teacher was his grandmother. She would come over and make brunch with Nick. By the time Nick was three, he would cook breakfast for his grandmother when she came over. At the time, he saw his grandmother cooking for his father, and his father cooking for him, so it seemed only right to cook for Grandma. Nick cooked for her until she died. After that, for the next few months, he felt as if he

*His return to the
kitchen, memorializing
his grandmother,
was an ambitious
meal of crab cakes,
stuffed quail, and an
assortment of side
dishes—all at the age
of ten…*

had no one to cook for. Several months after her passing, Nick's mom invited a friend over and Nick decided he wanted to cook dinner all by himself. His return to the kitchen, memorializing his grandmother, was an ambitious meal of crab cakes, stuffed quail, and an assortment of side dishes—all at the age of ten.

Nick is now 17, and his love for cooking hasn't diminished. He has several restaurants high on his list when he goes out to eat. If Nick is being treated to dinner, he chooses Camino, a restaurant that highlights simple cooking techniques and the freshest local ingredients. When Nick is paying, you are more likely to find him scarfing down a Fried Molé and Plantain Burrito at Baja Taqueria on Piedmont Avenue. He also loves the Hot and Sour Soup or the Mongolian Beef at Little Shin Shin, on the same street.

One of the local events Nick tries not to miss is the East Bay Bike Party, held monthly. Bicyclists commonly congregate around Lake Merritt, or West Oakland BART, and hundreds of riders roll through the city, celebrating their freedom to gather over a common love for biking. This event is a great example of what Nick loves about Oakland. When Nick recently did this ride, he saw people coming in from all parts of Oakland, and from all different backgrounds, no one too cool to talk to someone else.

As we talk, Nick gently folds parmesan into the creamy and light ricotta dough he is making, dusting the mixture with just enough flour to bring the cheeses together. We stand in the kitchen, watching him lay sage down in his pan atop browning butter, and carefully forming small rolls of gnocchi, which he drops into a large pot of boiling water steaming on the stovetop. As Nick works his way through the kitchen, bending to reach the countertop, he is just as excited to cook as he was on those long ago days when his grandmother would come over for brunch.

RICOTTA GNOCCHI

Yields 4-6 portions

Gnocchi

1 pound ricotta

1 ⅓ cups finely grated Parmesan cheese

2 eggs, whisked

1 cup flour

Salt and pepper

Sage butter

4 tablespoons butter

8-10 sage leaves

DIRECTIONS

For forming the gnocchi

In a medium bowl mix the ricotta and parmesan, folding to combine well. Add the eggs and stir until very well combined and the mixture has a uniform color. Add ½ of the flour and fold to combine.

Bring a medium pot of water to a gentle boil and add a big pinch of salt.

Form a 1 tablespoon ball of dough. Roll it between your palms to make a 1 inch long log. Drop the test gnocchi into the boiling water. If the gnocchi does not hold together, add another sprinkle of flour, incorporate, and test another one. As soon as the gnocchi holds together, while it is still light and fluffy, stop adding flour.

Now that the batter is right, turn off the boiling water and refrigerate the gnocchi batter (1-3 hours) to make the forming process easy.

Form all the gnocchi, bring the water back to a boil, and drop batches into the pot. When the gnocchi float to the surface of the water (45-60 seconds) they are finished and can be transferred with a slotted spoon to a serving dish.

For the sage butter

While the gnocchi are cooking, melt the butter in a small pan over high heat. Add the sage, and cook until crisp and the butter solids at the bottom of the pan are beginning to turn golden brown (1-2 minutes).

Pour a generous helping of sage butter over the gnocchi and finish with cracked black pepper. Serve immediately.

WONTON NOODLE
SOUP

LONGFELLOW, OAKLAND NU

You may be surprised by the simple mellow flavors of this soup. Surprised, that is, until you mix sriracha, fish sauce, and hoisin into the steaming hot broth. As the fiery chili pepper and the sweet pungent molasses of the hoisin disperse into the soup, it will all begin to make sense. When you become comfortable with this recipe, adapt it to your taste. The bok choy can serve as a placeholder for any of your favorite Asian vegetables.

NGAN-HA HO, KNOWN AS NU by friends, lives in Oakland's Longfellow neighborhood, right off of Martin Luther King Jr. Way. Longfellow is quiet and peaceful, with an occasional interruption from a passing truck or fire siren. When we joined her in her kitchen, Nu was filling dumplings, boiling a large pot of daikon root vegetable stock, frying little ringlets of pearl onion, sautéing bok choy, and straining noodles—all the while claiming she didn't cook much.

Nu grew up in Danang, a large port city on the coast of central Vietnam. Her father and mother were both high school teachers. Her father taught math and science, and her mother taught Vietnamese literature. After the Communist Party took control, they moved to Rach Gia, a sleepy fishing town in the southern region of the country. They built a palm leaf cottage from the ground up and sowed their land parcel with sweet potatoes, watermelons, and rice. In their new town, Nu and her family woke up each day to the sound of vendors walking through the streets, and the pungent smell of

They built a palm leaf cottage from the ground up and sowed their land parcel with sweet potatoes, watermelons, and rice…

fish sauce and pickled goods. After breakfast, the family would stroll through the open market, buying the fresh ingredients that would go into that day's lunch and dinner.

This move was part of an escape plan. Nu's father abandoned his old life, creating a new name and picking up a new profession—fishing. Over the next several years, as he learned to fish, he found like-minded people who were willing to contribute funds to help him build a boat. He and the other escapees were to take this boat on a nighttime fishing trip and flee to Thailand, where they could arrange their next move.

When Nu was 13, the boat was finished and her father was ready to push off. He took one of Nu's brothers, as well as her uncle, and two other boys. Nu, her other siblings, and her mother were set to take a small taxi boat to meet her father in the ocean when the sun went down and darkness had set in. If they could not reach him in time he would have to leave without them; otherwise his boat would be intercepted by the Coast Guard, and everything they had worked for would be thrown away.

Nu, her siblings, and her mother got on their boat, but were apprehended by the Coast Guard. The rendezvous time crept closer and then passed. Nu's father was gone—as far as they knew—forever.

As it turned out, his boat was intercepted by pirates. The pirates poured rice in his engine to keep him from giving chase. Without any power to move the boat, he used his knowledge of the stars and slowly steered the boat in the direction of land. Nu and her family spent the next several months fearing the worst. Eventually they received a telegram: Nu's father was finally safe in Thailand and was working on bringing them to join him.

He spent the next decade working through various visas and citizenship requests for Nu and her family. Ten years from the time they had missed their rendezvous in that dark ocean, they were all reunited in San Jose, California. This was the first time Nu had seen her father since the treacherous night when so much had gone wrong at sea.

A couple of years later, when Nu was settling into her new life, she met Jack, her future husband, in the dark-room at Academy of Art College in San Francisco where she was majoring in photography. Together they moved to Oakland. The longer Nu lived with Jack, the more interested she became in cooking. As Jack, a restaurant chef, took Nu around Oakland on food adventures, she began to appreciate the diversity of Oakland's food scene. While Nu may say Jack is the only chef in the family, that is not how it appears: three pans and a pot sizzle and boil on the stove, as she and her daughter, Sông-An, work around the kitchen together.

When Nu visits Rạch Giá, the town where she grew up, it is no longer a quiet, serene fishing town. Vietnam has rushed to keep up with a quickly developing world, and many of Nu's memories of an old life were swept away with this industrial development. In Vietnam, this is called "Lấn Biển" which translates to pushing the ocean back. The meaning behind the phrase is that, as cities rush to fit more and more people, they push the water back to make more space for homes and high rises. The hustle and bustle of busy life have swept the peaceful calm out of the fresh sea air.

Nu and Jack usually eat at home, but when they go out, it is often to Xyclo, a Vietnamese restaurant that uses seasonal produce for inspiration. During the day Nu can be found greeting regular customers at her husband's restaurant, Aunt Mary's Cafe, in the Temescal neighborhood, or hanging out around the house. After living through war, pirates, and midnight escapes, Nu Ho has made a beautiful home in Oakland, California.

WONTON NOODLE SOUP

Yields 5-8 portions, 30-40 wontons
Extra wontons can be frozen and cooked later.

Stock

2-3 inches ginger, peeled, sliced in thin rounds

2 medium onions, peeled, cut in half

1 medium (1 pound) daikon, chopped roughly

2 large carrots, chopped roughly

½ red onion, peeled

3 leek tops, rinsed

2 ½ teaspoons salt

Wontons

Vegetable oil, for frying

3 leeks, sliced thinly and rinsed in a colander

½ red onion, peeled and chopped finely

1 pound button mushrooms, chopped finely

¼ inch fresh ginger, peeled and grated

1 teaspoon salt

½ teaspoon Chinese five spice powder

Cornstarch, for dusting

1 package circular wheat wonton wrappers

Garnish and assembly

Vegetable oil, for frying

5 red pearl onions, peeled and sliced thinly

½ pound fresh thin cut wheat noodles

1 ½ pounds bok choy, halved lengthwise and rinsed

2 green onions, peeled and chopped into thin rounds

Sriracha

Hoisin

Fish sauce

DIRECTIONS

For the stock

Preheat the oven to 350 degrees.

Roast the ginger and onions in the oven for 30 minutes until golden brown. Add 3 ½ quarts of water to a large pot. Add the daikon, carrots, red onion, roasted onions, roasted ginger, leek tops, and salt. Simmer at medium low heat for 1-2 hours, until the stock is golden brown and flavorful. Strain the vegetables out and discard. Set the stock aside in the pot.

For the wontons

Heat ¼ cup vegetable oil in a high-sided pan over medium heat. Add the leeks and red onion and cook until neither are crisp and they have begun to steam and break down (5-10 minutes). Add the mushrooms, ginger, salt, and Chinese five spice. Cook until mushrooms are tender and any excess water in the bottom of the pan has cooked off (5-7 minutes). Remove from heat and taste for salt and pepper.

Sift cornstarch evenly onto a large sheet tray to coat the bottom. Spoon a heaping teaspoon of filling into the middle of a wonton wrapper. Fold in half and cinch the two sides together by pressing and pleating with a fork or with your fingers. Place on the tray. Continue until you have used all of the filling.

For the garnish

Add ¼ inch vegetable oil to a small pot or high-sided pan and set to medium heat. Test the heat of the oil by putting a sliver of pearl onion into the oil. When it sizzles and pops, add the rest of the sliced pearl onions and fry until lightly browned (2–5 minutes). Remove to a paper towel to drain.

Assembly

Boil water in a medium pot and generously salt water. Add the noodles, stirring occasionally until cooked but still slightly chewy (3–4 minutes). Strain the noodles and set aside. In the same pot boil the bok choy until tender but still green (2–3 minutes).

Bring the stock to a boil and add the sliced green onions. In batches put wontons in the stock. When they rise back to the top of the pot and are translucent, they are done (3–5 minutes).

To serve, place a portion of noodles in the middle of each bowl. Add several wontons, and place the bok choy around the noodles and wontons, along with a ladle of broth.

Garnish with fried pearl onions.

Enjoy with sriracha, hoisin, and fish sauce to bring all the flavors to life. The soup is very light and is an excellent carrier for your favorite sweet and spicy condiments.

CATFISH & CANDIED YAMS

MEADOW BROOK, OAKLAND KIM

Soul food recipes are typically passed down through the family, just as Kim's have been. Measurements change from time to time, so feel free to add an extra dash of this or sprinkle of that. When you do have a chance to cook and enjoy a plate of fried catfish and candied yams, or hushpuppies, or oxtails, or cornbread and fried chicken, or black-eyed peas, be prepared to fall deeply in love with the process, from start to finish.

RIGHT OFF OF BUSTLING Foothill Boulevard, surrounded by beauty parlors, taco trucks, a quinceañera supply store, and dozens of other small family businesses, Kim lives in the Meadow Brook neighborhood. On first appearance, it is clear Kim does not go for normal. Bright pink hair, a large pink purse, and matching shoes make up her signature look. She was born in Fresno, but moved around as a kid, and lived in Berkeley, Emeryville, and Oakland. Her parents were both from the South—her mother from Mississippi and her father from Louisiana. She grew up with a lot of what she described as "Southern comfort"—a sense of soulful pride, and the Southern dishes her family brought here with them.

Kim was always interested in cooking. Her mother was never one to measure, so Kim would follow behind, noting measurements for the recipes, so she could recreate the dishes on her own. Fried Catfish and Candied Purple Yams are two of Kim's favorites. It quickly became clear why, as we watched candied yams slowly bubbling away on a back burner, their sugars concentrating. As Kim effortlessly flipped the fish,

As Kim effortlessly flipped the fish, its crust became perfectly browned. We were tempted to grab some, scorching hot, and break a flaking piece right off, "just to test it…"

we were tempted to grab some, scorching hot, and break a flaking piece right off, "just to test it."

As a child, Kim did not go a day without the Southern food her mother had grown up with. Back then, on New Year's Eve in Oakland, the house was filled with the aroma of braising greens, black-eyed peas, and roasting ham. On Thanksgiving, the overwhelming scent of rosemary gravy over Pan Cornbread poured from the kitchen.

Kim moved to Oakland over 30 years ago. She has pleasant memories of growing up here, recalling how all her neighbors looked out for each other and made sure none of the kids were getting in trouble or doing anything foolish. Kim has five sons of her own now, four of whom cook. Kim and her mother were always in the kitchen together, and Kim's sons would help out and learn, just as Kim had done when she was a child. Phillip, one of her sons, was so interested in cooking he decided to do it as a career. He was given a scholarship to go to culinary school. Kim joked that Philip's sweet potato pie is so delicious his grandma would rise out of the grave if she tasted it.

More than anything else, Kim has always loved to cook for her family and friends, and it always makes for a full house. She cooks large dinners on many of the holidays. When she tells one of her relatives she is going to make dinner, they will pass the word on: Kyma tells Adrell, Adrell tells Mimi and Mama Sista. Kim recounted all the favorite dishes her family liked to eat. "Nicholas likes my Jambalaya with lots of shrimps. He loves my greens. Christopher loves Mac and Cheese and Fried Chicken. Melvin loves everything, and my grandbabies love Nana's Banana Pudding."

Kim's church has also been blessed with her cooking. Since the time they first tried one of her dishes at a potluck, the pastor and his wife have asked her to cook something at all of their events. Kim is sometimes recognized as she is walking around Oakland because of her reputation as a cook at church and local potlucks. "This is the chicken lady, I heard you have the best fried chicken in Oakland," is not an unusual opening line from a stranger on the street.

On holidays, Kim is at her church serving up soul food to the homeless people in the neighborhood—smoked turkey, regular turkey, dressing, yams, and green beans— a menu which is bound to draw a line of people around the block. When anyone tries to pay Kim for her cooking service, she tells them it is not about the money. Seeing people's smiles and satisfaction has sufficed.

Kim moved across the Bay to San Francisco for some time, but when her mother got sick she moved back to Oakland to take care of her. Her mom, the one who had taught her how to cook soul food and cook from the heart, now needed to eat a new kind of food. When her mom got sick, Kim had to start cooking foods that did not have a lot of sugar or oil in them. She dedicated her time to taking care of her mother and making sure all her meals were healthy and nutritious. Although her mother protested, fried catfish and candied yams took the back burner, while the braised collard greens and black-eyed peas were set on the table.

"Soul food is from the heart. It's like a passion that you have to love to do. Especially when you're putting in your ingredients, it's the love that you're putting in there. It comes from the heart."

CATFISH AND CANDIED YAMS

Yields 4-6 portions

Both the yams and the catfish require a resting period of at least 2 hours before they can be cooked. Plan on starting this meal several hours before you intend to sit and eat.

Catfish

4 catfish filets, about ¾ pound each

1 (6 ounce) bottle Crystal hot sauce

1 teaspoon garlic powder

1 teaspoon black pepper

Vegetable oil, for frying

Fine ground yellow cornmeal, for dredging

Yams

2 pounds (5-6 small) purple yams

1 ½ cups sugar

2 teaspoons vanilla extract

1 teaspoon lemon juice + ¼ of the lemon's zest

1 tablespoon nutmeg

1 (4 ounce) stick butter

DIRECTIONS

For the yams

Peel the yams thoroughly so that all that is left is the purple flesh. The white exterior is tough and will not break down. Soak the yams in cool water for at least 2 hours, allowing them to become tender.

Slice the yams into thick finger size sticks. In a small pot over low heat mix the yams, sugar, vanilla extract, lemon juice, zest, nutmeg, and all of the butter. Combine well and cover with a lid. Stir every 15 minutes, ensuring the yams are cooking evenly. When the yams are very soft and the sugars are almost all absorbed, turn the pot off (30-40 minutes). Leave the pot covered to keep the yams warm until the catfish is ready.

For the catfish

Marinate the catfish filets in enough of the hot sauce to dredge both sides and marinate for 2 hours in the refrigerator.

Season the catfish filets with garlic powder and ground black pepper. Heat a large cast iron pan over medium heat, and add ⅓ inch vegetable oil. Put cornmeal in a large wide bowl or shallow container. Toss a small sprinkle of cornmeal into the oil. When it fizzes and floats to the top, turn the heat to medium low.

Remove the catfish from the hot sauce and allow excess liquid to drain off. Dredge the catfish filets in cornmeal, making sure they are completely coated. Fit as many filets in the pan as you can without them crowding and touching. Fry for 5-7 minutes on the first side, until the crust is golden brown. Carefully flip the fish, using 2 spatulas or a set of tongs.

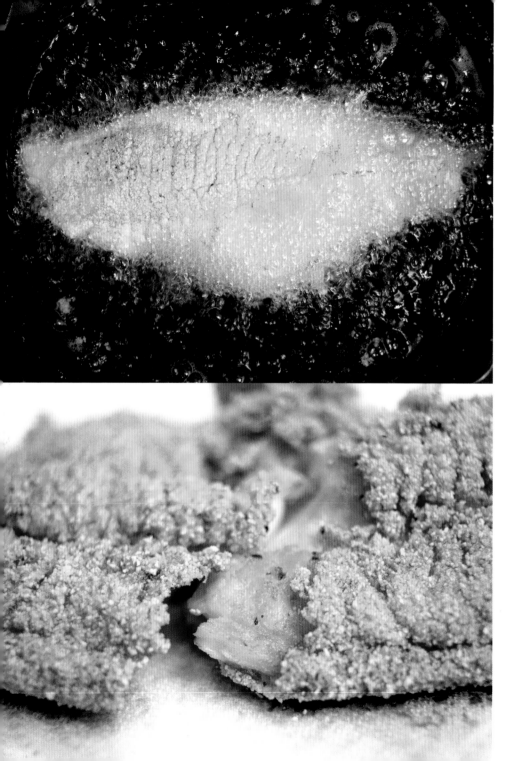

Cook for another 4-6 minutes until the second side has reached the same golden brown as the first. Remove the fish to a plate with several layers of paper towels and let rest for 5-6 minutes.

Enjoy with Crystal hot sauce and a big serving of candied yams.

LAU LAU
WOODMINSTER, OAKLAND   TONY

Most of your preparation for these Lau Lau will happen the night before you want to eat, salting the pork and fish ahead of time so the flavor is rich and full. By the time you come back to finish wrapping your Lau Lau and setting them to steam the next morning, there is almost nothing left to do but sit to unwrap the steaming banana leaves and enjoy.

AS OUR CAR PUTTERED and climbed slowly up the winding streets to Tony's house, the scenery became increasingly green and the noise of the city shrank away. By the time we reached his house, we almost forgot we had been in the bustle of downtown Oakland only a few minutes earlier.

Tony lives in a tall old house in the Woodminster neighborhood of the Oakland Hills. As we strolled down the pathway towards the front door, Tony could be seen through the steaming kitchen window in a bright floral shirt, preparing Lau Lau and Poi, dishes he grew up eating. Poi is a paste made of taro root, mashed until it becomes viscous and smooth. Tony laughed as he initially explained that, to him, Poi was like mother's milk. When breastfeeding was not popular in the 60's, his mother consulted with Hawaiian elders, who recommended she mix poi with the baby formula. It was his first food.

Although Tony was born and raised in Hawaii, he is not ethnically Hawaiian. Tony's mother and father moved to Hawaii before he was born. As Tony heard it, his father had been assigned a position at a United States radar base during the Cold War and he was set to be transferred to Tully, Greenland because of his troublemaking. He heard of this move the night before, bought a bottle of whisky for the man writing

up transfer locations, and was mysteriously on his way to Hawaii the next morning. Tony's mother, wanting to put some few thousand miles between her and her family, became a nurse at Queens Hospital in Honolulu.

In his kitchen, Tony talked with the air of someone in no rush to get anywhere fast, as he unfolded huge banana leaves. We were given plenty of time to relax and enjoy each other's company while the pork slowly steamed away. By 10 pm it had become clear that, regardless of Tony's ethnic background, he had island time in his DNA.

Tony's father became a businessman after he got out of the military. He traveled a lot, searching for new get-rich-quick schemes. Tony's mother raised Tony, his brother, and his little sister. His mother became truly interested in food after moving to Hawaii, and learned to cook dishes from all the different cuisines available on the islands— Lumpia, Inari, all kinds of fresh fish. When she worked at the hospital, all of the nurses brought in dishes and shared cooking techniques and stories. Tony would get to try these dishes when his mother recreated them at home.

By the early 60's, things in Hawaii were beginning to change. A new drug culture was taking hold and the beaches were filled with traveling stoners. Tony's parents did not like this change, and his father spotted potential business ventures in Fiji. He was certain Fiji was going to be "the next Hawaii." It did not turn out to hold the opportunities he had anticipated, but the family lived there for six years, nevertheless. Three of these years Tony spent in an Australian boarding school, because there were few educational opportunities on Fiji. Through all these changes and moves, Tony's mother kept learning to cook different kinds of food and Tony kept watching. In Fiji,

Tony's house was always filled with the smell of sweet and spicy chutneys and bubbling curries from the large Indian influence on the island.

By the time Tony was in high school, the family had moved again, this time back to the mainland in Concord, California. During Tony's time in college, at San Francisco State, a friend who was obsessed with puppets got him a summer job at Oakland's Fairyland. Tony was finishing school and had decided to enlist in the Peace Corps and go back to Fiji. Those plans changed when he met his future wife, Kelly, the sister of his friend's girlfriend. Tony and Kelly moved around the Bay Area, but not immediately to Oakland, Kelly's hometown. It was when Kelly's mother passed away that they ended up back in Kelly's childhood house. They first moved there to take care of her father, and stayed to raise both of their daughters.

Although Tony and Kelly sometimes think about the prospect of packing up after their daughters leave for college, and beginning their travels again, it would be awfully hard for them to leave Oakland. Until that day comes, Tony and Kelly have plenty of places to eat and enjoy, from Koryo Jajang, a Korean Barbecue restaurant on Telegraph, to the taquerias dispersed throughout East Oakland, such as Los Comales in the Dimond District.

It has been 40 years since Tony reached the mainland, but he still lives each day with the calm of someone who spent a childhood on the beaches of Hawaii. And he still finds the time to make the dishes, Lau Lau included, that bring him back to his days spent playing in the soft sand and warm water of the islands.

In Fiji, Tony's house was always filled with the smell of sweet and spicy chutneys and bubbling curries from the large Indian influence on the island…

LAU LAU

Yields 8 Lau Lau

Taro leaves and fresh banana leaves are available at 99 Ranch Market (Richmond).

The Lau Lau must rest and absorb salt for at least 8 hours and cook for 6-7 hours. If the cooking time does not align with your next meal time, you can steam or boil the parcels to reheat them. If you can only fit 4 Lau Lau in your steamer basket the recipe can easily be cut in half.

¾ pound pork belly, cut into 8 equally sized cubes

1 ½ pounds pork shoulder, cut into 8 equally sized cubes

3 tablespoons salt

½ pound butterfish, sliced in 8 equally sized filets

25 medium sized taro leaves

1 package fresh banana leaves

Twine

DIRECTIONS

In a medium bowl mix the pork belly and shoulder with 2 tablespoons of the salt. In a separate bowl season the fish filets with the third tablespoon of salt. Rest the fish and pork for 8-12 hours in the refrigerator.

Later, bring water to a gentle boil in the bottom of a steam basket or steamer fan.

Slice the stems off of the taro leaves and rinse the leaves gently. Stack two taro leaves on top of each other on a clean surface. Put a piece of pork belly, a piece of pork shoulder, and a piece of fish in the center of the stacked leaves.

Roll the leaves up, folding the sides under to seal the package. Cut banana leaves into 8 12-inch squares. Quickly run each of the banana leaves over a high flame on the stove to soften them. With the shiny side facing down towards the countertop, place the pork and fish package in the middle of the banana leaf. Wrap carefully, attempting to tear the banana leaf as little as possible. If the banana leaf rips, just remove the taro package and try again with a new leaf. Tie a piece of twine around the package like a present so the whole banana leaf is securely wrapped. Repeat this process with all 8 parcels.

Place the Lau Lau in the steamer and cook for 6-7 hours. Make sure every hour that the water in the bottom of the steamer has not boiled off.

The Lau Lau are done when the fat has rendered and the pork can be easily pulled apart with a fork.

Enjoy with steamed white rice.

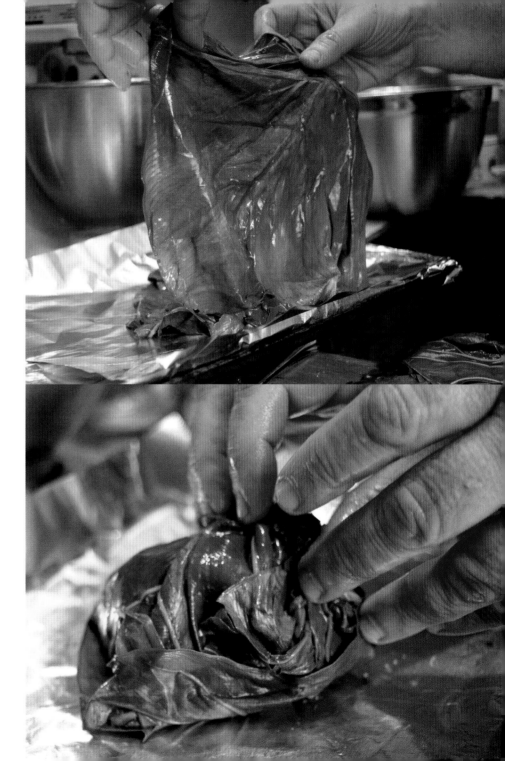

CRAB CURRY

TRESTLE GLEN, OAKLAND   JACKIE & REBECCA

Sitting perched over Jackie and Rebecca's marble countertop, bib around your neck, be prepared to try some new things. If you were reared on forks, spoons, and knives, it is hard not to break down and giggle at yourself as you realize how terribly inexperienced you have become at eating with your hands. Conversation is light and lively, and this is the most peaceful and satisfying moment you have had in a long time — regardless of how much curry paste and crab juice are dribbling down your new white shirt.

ON A SUNNY DAY IN OAKLAND, after a walk around Lake Merritt, we headed up the hill to Rebecca and Jackie's house. Shortly after we arrived, Rebecca, Jackie's oldest daughter, returned from 99 Ranch Market, an Asian grocery store where she frequently shops. In her bag she carried crabs, lemongrass, and coconut milk for the curry she and her mother were going to teach us to cook. Mother and daughter bantered happily as they chopped onions, crushed garlic, and peeled ginger. The fresh crabs were cooked in a light, creamy sauce, flavored with herbs from the backyard, and served over steaming brown rice. When plated, Rebecca showed us how the curry and rice were to be picked up and eaten with the thumb, index, middle, and ring fingers of the right hand.

Jackie was born in Tanzania, where her father was getting a civil engineering degree, but her family is from Goa, a coastal town in India, known in the U.S. for its festive parties and ex-pat hippy culture. The traditional diet in Goa consists of fresh seafood, rich curries, crab dishes, and a myriad of meats and vegetables. Jackie and her husband have kept that tradition alive.

Her husband, Jonathan, is from Kandy, Sri Lanka. They live with their two youngest daughters in a beautiful house in the Trestle Glen neighborhood. The garden

behind the house scales the hilly terrain above and to the east of Lake Merritt, and this is where Jackie grows the fresh curry leaves she uses to make her curries.

Twenty-one years ago, Jackie and her husband moved to Oakland. They both held jobs in Silicon Valley, but loved Oakland and decided it was worth the daily commute. Jackie looks back on her first years in Oakland, and remembers when the police would shut down Lake Merritt at night due to the gang presence. In recent years, both Jackie and Rebecca have watched the lake become a safe and festive place to hang out nearly any time of day.

Rebecca,19, is studying at UC Berkeley, and has been very active in Oakland's youth initiatives. She went to Oakland School for the Arts, and that is where she began to see Oakland change in ways that concern her. In the years that Rebecca attended the school, she saw that population go from a mixed and diverse group of kids to "almost completely white." Rebecca witnessed drastic changes in the historic downtown as well. Rebecca loves many of the new downtown establishments, such as Duende, a Basque restaurant, and she hopes that newcomers will participate in the complex and colorful culture that already exists in Oakland, rather than trying to create 'new culture'.

The love among the family members in Jackie's house is impossible to miss. And if Jackie feels that Rebecca hasn't been home enough, she sends her a text and tells her that beef stew or crab curry is on the stove for dinner. This makes for a guaranteed return home. Rebecca laughingly admits that she comes home two or three times a week to eat with her family. Both Sri Lankan and Indian cultures center around the sharing of food. A dinner could easily consist of six or seven dishes, all freshly prepared, with a mixture of fresh vegetables and meats. Rebecca and Jackie explained that for the

Indians and Sri Lankans, faced with the turmoil of colonization and war, one of the main ways of retaining culture was through the sharing of recipes and food. Mother and daughter are both very tied in to their culture and ancestry, and one of the main connections remains the food they cook and eat.

When neither Jackie nor Rebecca wants to cook, they rely on the fare offered at one of their Oakland favorites, like Kamdesh, an Afghan restaurant offering delicious food in a homey environment, or Ba Le, a Vietnamese restaurant with a favorite dish of theirs—Beef Bun Bo Xao and fried rolls. Though representing different cultures, these restaurants capture the tastes of home cooking that Jackie and Rebecca love.

But most days, Jackie cooks. So, if you see a mother and daughter walking through the Asian market with crabs in one hand and lemongrass in the other, you may want to try striking up a conversation and wrangle an invitation to dinner. This is a meal you will not forget.

The garden behind the house scales the hilly terrain above and to the east of Lake Merritt, and this is where Jackie grows the fresh curry leaves she uses to make her curries…

JAFFNA CRAB CURRY

Yields 6-8 portions

All the ingredients except Jaffna Curry Powder can be purchased at Berkeley Bowl or 99 Ranch Asian Market.

If you are not keen on killing and cleaning the crabs yourself, your local fishmonger would be happy to do so for you.

The Jaffna Curry Powder recipe is listed below. Serve with brown rice, eat with your hands, and have a bib at the ready!

Jaffna Curry Powder

Yields 4 tablespoons

2 tablespoons crushed red chili flakes

1 tablespoon ground coriander

½ teaspoon whole black peppercorns

½ teaspoon cumin seed

1 heaping teaspoon fennel seed

¼ teaspoon fenugreek seed

1 (1-inch) piece of turmeric, peeled and sliced thinly

10 fresh curry leaves

Coffee grinder or spice grinder or mortar and pestle

Curry

Olive oil, for pan frying

1 onion, chopped finely

1 inch ginger, peeled and sliced into thin strips

6 cloves garlic, peeled and chopped roughly

4 Roma tomatoes, chopped finely

10 fresh curry leaves

2 teaspoons salt

1 tablespoon fish sauce

1 tablespoon tamarind paste

3 tablespoons Jaffna Curry Powder (from above)

1 stalk lemon grass, tough tops and outer layer discarded, light interior cut into 2-3 inch pieces

2 teaspoons brown sugar

¾ cup sweet chili sauce

1 (13 ½ ounce) can coconut milk (about 1 ⅔ cup)

4 Dungeness crabs (1 ¾-2 pounds each), cleaned and quartered

DIRECTIONS

For the curry powder

In a small pan over high heat, toast the chili flakes, coriander, black pepper, cumin, fennel seed, and fenugreek seed. Move the spices constantly, until the mixture begins to pop and the fragrance is strong (1-2 minutes). Finely grind the spices and set aside.

In the same pan toast the turmeric to draw out some of the moisture (2-3 minutes). Repeat with the curry leaves, toasting them until dry and just browned on the edges (1-2 minutes). Finely grind the curry leaves and turmeric. Mix the ground dried spices with the fresh spices you have prepared.

For the curry

Heat a large, high-sided pan or wok over medium heat, and add enough oil to coat the bottom. Add the onion, ginger, and garlic and cook until the onion has become translucent and the ginger is fragrant (8-10 minutes).

Add the tomatoes and fresh curry leaves. The flavors will begin to mellow out and work together as the fresh curry leaves and tomatoes meld into the curry base (5-10 minutes).

Add the salt, fish sauce, tamarind paste, curry powder, lemongrass, and brown sugar. Make sure the tamarind paste and sugar melt into the mix and incorporate well. Add the sweet chili paste.

Taste and make sure there is a good balance of spice, acidity, and sweetness. You can increase the spiciness of the dish by adding some more chili paste. If you find that you have added a little too much, add ¼ teaspoon of fish sauce and taste again. This curry should hold a subtle sweetness with a kick of spice. When the flavors are to your liking, add the coconut milk and bring the mixture to a gentle simmer over medium low heat.

Carefully place the crab pieces in the bubbling curry. Turn and coat the crabs in the curry mixture, ladling some over the top. It is okay if the tops of the legs stick out of the mixture as long as a lid can be put on the pan or wok. Cover and simmer over low heat, checking after 5-6 minutes. Flip the crabs if they are not completely immersed and cook for another 5 minutes, or until the crab meat flakes when it is poked with a toothpick or a skewer.

Transfer the curry to shallow bowls and enjoy over rice.

M&M CHALLAH

ALLENDALE, OAKLAND   RUTH

This is not the challah your bubbie grew up making. Nor is it the challah you should make when your Orthodox girlfriend or boyfriend's parents come over for their first Shabbat at your house. Those are the only times you may not want to make this challah. Any other time, it's a go. Turn on the light in your oven and watch as the coating on the chocolate slowly melts and bleeds into the dough, painting it a hilariously colorful mix of yellows, blues and reds.

RUTH'S HOUSE IS IN THE Allendale neighborhood of Oakland, on a dead-end road only a few steps from busy 35th Avenue, with Fruitvale on one side and MacArthur Boulevard on the other. As we walked up to her front door, the three large pit bulls in the neighbor's yard barked loudly, warning that newcomers had arrived. At the end of this cul-de-sac is an apartment building, with music blaring and lights on at nearly any time of the day or night. The neighbors' music is blocked out as soon as you go through the door leading into Ruth's cozy living room.

The aroma of bagels toasting, eggs frying in butter, chicken roasting, livers searing in a pan, or any of the other familiar smells Ruth recalls from her childhood, bring her back to the family dinner table she used to share with her twin sister, her older sister, and her parents. Growing up Jewish in Oakland, Ruth was always tuned in to her religious and cultural background. From preschool, she remembers making the same M&M challah that is now rising on her kitchen counter.

Thanks to her father, Judaism was braided into Ruth's everyday patterns. Every Friday night was Shabbat dinner at Ruth's house. The table was set, a chicken was roasted, the gizzards were broiled, potatoes were mashed, broccoli was steamed, and

*She found herself at
an unfamiliar table,
singing the same hymns
with a different melody,
trying to understand
her culture in a whole
new way…*

challah was eaten. Ruth was hard-pressed to remember a Friday with her parents that did not follow the same order every time.

Saturdays had a similarly consistent pattern: In the morning before Hebrew school, the girls would wake up to scrambled eggs, and toast made from last night's challah. Every day but Sunday had a meal plan at her parents' home. While her father and mother were cooking dinner, Ruth would sit on a stool and watch, asking questions the whole time. With the routine menu Ruth's mom and dad created, she began to look forward to certain flavors, dishes, and days of the week.

Now that Ruth is an adult and no longer lives at home, she sometimes visits her parents based on the menu. Monday, always pasta; stop by on a Thursday and there is piping hot pizza waiting for you from Cybelle's on Piedmont Avenue. Ruth's mother and father raised their children in a "kosher style." There was never bacon in the house, nor shrimp or crab, but Wednesday night's go-to dinner, Chicken Parmesan (a big no in strict kosher households because of the mixing of dairy and meat), was okay. Her Oakland household and community fostered a sense of Judaism that did not require Ruth to live within a strict set of laws.

Ruth attended college an hour outside of Los Angeles. The Judaism she had become so comfortable with in Oakland was missing in college. It was the little things. From not being able to find the right kind of matzah, to not recognizing the tunes of prayer songs she had grown up singing in Temple, she was unsettled and isolated. She found herself at an unfamiliar table, singing the same hymns with a different melody, trying to understand her culture in a whole new way.

After college, Ruth moved back to Oakland. When she was not working, she was fine-tuning her skills as a baker, creating elaborate cakes that embodied some characteristics of the people for whom she was making them— her "bagel cake," topped with jelly beans for capers, layers of fondant shaped and colored to artfully imitate onions and tomatoes; or the radio-shaped cake she created for her roommate, who is a pop singer and music aficionado.

If Ruth is not at her parents' house for Shabbat dinner, and she has not yet started a new cake design, she is likely to be on her way to Guadalajara, a taco truck very close to the Fruitvale BART station. She recommends, "If you're really hungry, you get a carne asada super burrito, you get limes, green salsa, radishes, scallions, and you die of happiness. If you want to keep going, you go to Colonial Doughnuts at midnight. It's fresh. It's amazing."

Ruth is most comfortable when everyone around her is well-fed and content. Whether you arrive for dinner on a Wednesday night or for challah on Shabbat, expect to be treated well and to leave full. Unless, that is, Ruth has decided she misses her parents, in which case she will be enjoying a steaming plate of Spaghetti and Red Sauce, or Lasagna if it's a lucky Monday night.

M & M CHALLAH

Yields 2 challahs

1 large (11.4 ounce) bag M & M's

1 cup warm water

¼ cup + 1 teaspoon sugar

1 package (2 ¼ teaspoons) active dry yeast

3 cups all purpose flour + extra for dusting surface

1 cup high gluten or bread flour

2 teaspoons salt

½ cup vegetable oil

3 eggs

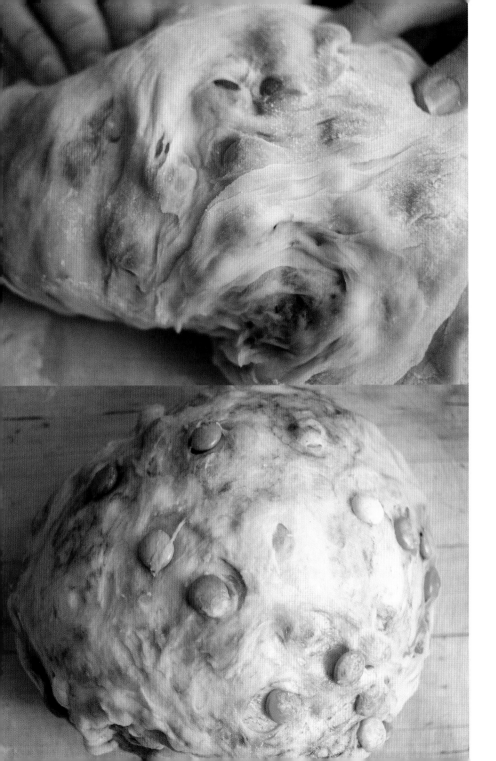

DIRECTIONS

Put the M & M's in the freezer.

In a medium bowl, mix ½ cup of the warm water and 1 teaspoon of the sugar and stir to combine. Add the yeast, mix lightly to immerse, and let stand until foamy (about 10 minutes).

In a medium bowl mix the all purpose flour with the high gluten flour and salt.

Mix the remaining sugar and water into the yeast mixture, along with the vegetable oil, and 2 of the eggs.

Incorporate the first two cups of flour into the yeast mixture. Mix in an electric mixer with a dough hook attachment or with a wooden spoon until the dough is well combined. The dough will still be very sticky and glutinous. Slowly add the rest of the flour as you continue to mix. Transfer the dough to a large bowl and cover with a damp thin towel. Make sure the towel is not touching the top of the dough and allow to rest for 10 minutes.

Flour a large work surface and transfer the dough onto the work surface. Rinse out and lightly oil the mixing bowl. Knead the dough until it is very smooth and workable (8-10 minutes). You may have to dust with flour as you knead for the first several minutes as the dough will still be sticky. Return the well-kneaded dough to the oiled bowl. Dust the top of the dough with flour and punch it down with your knuckles. Cover with the damp towel and rest for 1 hour, in which time it will double in size.

Lay the dough back onto the floured surface, flatten it, and add ½ of the M & M's. Fold the dough over, flatten again, and add the second half of the M & M's. Knead the dough until the M & M's are fully distributed, working quickly so they melt as little as

possible. Roll the dough into a ball and divide into 6 equal-sized pieces. You will most likely have some M & M casualties when dividing the dough; they can be poked back into the individual balls.

Braiding the Challah

Preheat the oven to 400 degrees.

Take 3 of the balls and roll each one into a 12 inch long, 1 inch thick log. With water, wet one tip on each of the 3 logs, and squeeze the 3 tips together to connect. Braid tightly and connect the braid with a final dab of water to seal the 3 pieces together.

Repeat to form the second challah.

On an oiled baking tray, cover both challahs with a dry towel and rest for 20 minutes.

Whisk the remaining egg and liberally brush the tops and sides of both challahs.

Bake for 20–25 minutes until golden brown and beautiful.

Allow the challahs to rest until slightly warm and serve with butter.

SALMON WASABI BURGER

ALLENDALE, OAKLAND   PRINCETON

This salmon burger lies somewhere on the food matrix between a quick burger and a fancy dinner out. The salmon, adorned with a heaping serving of fresh arugula, is just fancy enough to make up for the deliciously plain Hawaiian sweet bun, and the bun is just casual enough to make this A-OK for a barbecue. The wasabi mayonnaise, well, that's just delicious.

AFTER VISITING RUTH'S HOUSE in the Allendale neighborhood for her M & M challah, we were compelled to return and cook with Princeton, her roommate and close friend. If you ever wondered whether the television shows about roommates going through life together are real, they are. Princeton, his boyfriend Vern, and Ruth have created a home that really could be Oakland's next big show.

On this visit, Princeton ushered us into his living room, sporting a large fanny pack, shorts above the knee, bleached blond hair, and brightly painted nails. A large bouncy couch dominates the living room, tempting everyone to give up their plans for the rest of the day and sink into comfiness. This is not a house that offers much peace and quiet. Princeton, Vern, and Ruth keep an open and welcoming home. Whether they are having a Sunday mimosa brunch or a weeknight dinner, there is likely to be a guest or two at the table. While Vern is catching his favorite TV show on the big couch, Princeton is likely in the kitchen pacing back and forth on the phone having an

His voice pumped through the car speakers singing of love, self-acceptance, and heartbreak. If you have not yet heard Princeton's CD, give it a listen…

energized and heated conversation about his new album while Ruth bakes one of her custom cakes.

The dish Princeton made for us was nothing like the food he grew up eating. A salmon burger is his take on a classic hamburger. Understanding the value of his food, both health and price-wise, Princeton is careful and meticulous as he cooks, giving each ingredient the respect it deserves. We accompanied him to Farmer Joe's, a local produce market, where he picked out the freshest and best-looking salmon filets he could find. He walked through each aisle, explaining why he uses the specific ingredients he does, from the red onions to the wasabi. We hopped back in the car and turned on *The Consummation*, Princeton's new album. His voice pumped through the car speakers singing of love, self-acceptance, and heartbreak. If you have not yet heard Princeton's CD, give it a listen, or check out his performance at Oakland's Gay Pride parade. We finished listening to the first few tracks and headed back inside.

At the house, Vern had already boiled a pot of water for the potato salad he was making to accompany our burgers. After skinning the fish and rinsing it gently under cool water, Princeton seasoned it with a combination of spices and herbs and laid it down in a hot cast iron pan.

Although Princeton loves to cook, it is not his calling. He has been interested in music for a very long time. From a young age, he took any opportunity that came his way to be on a stage or in a recording booth. At 12, he was part of an anti-drug singing group that went across the city performing at schools and encouraging fellow students to make good choices. From that innocent, good-natured message he offered 14 years ago, to the bright and emotionally charged pop he makes now, Princeton's music is a crucial part of his story.

Growing up as a gay black Yemeni boy in Oakland, things were not always easy for Princeton. He never tried to hide who he was to make others more comfortable. But Princeton's house at 66th Avenue, around the corner from the Coliseum, was always a long bus ride from wherever he was trying to go. Princeton laughed as he told us he was "hella gay," even as a young kid. He was never ashamed of himself but feared others' ignorance would cause him harm. Taking the bus was a challenge every day.

Princeton did not cook when he was young. It was not until several years ago that he found cooking, as a way to nurture his body and be healthy. Not growing up with a lot of financial breathing room, it was rarely an option for the family to go out to eat, so it made sense for Princeton to learn to cook. As it became clearer that what he ate affected him, he changed his diet and learned to make new dishes.

As Princeton has gotten older, his appreciation for the city's diversity has grown. When he leaves Oakland, he quickly notices the lack of gay business owners, gay politicians, and general pride that are so present in Oakland. When Princeton's day off lands on a Tuesday or Sunday, he might kick back his feet and enjoy five dollar movie night at Jack London Square. Or he may just stay home for a salmon burger and some of Vern's potato salad.

SALMON WASABI BURGER

Yields 4 burgers

1 large slicing tomato

1 large red onion

2 teaspoons garlic powder

2 teaspoons dried basil

1 teaspoon sweet smoked paprika

½ teaspoon cayenne

2 teaspoons salt

1 (1 ½ pound) salmon filet, skin removed

2 big handfuls arugula (¼ pound), rinsed and dried

4 Hawaiian sweet rolls

Vegetable oil, for pan frying

½ cup mayonnaise

2 teaspoons wasabi paste

DIRECTIONS

With a serrated knife slice the tomato into thick (¼ inch) rounds and cut the red onion into thin rounds.

Combine the garlic powder, dried basil, paprika, cayenne and salt, and taste for balance. Make sure there is enough salt and a little spice.

Section the salmon into 4 filets of equal size and season with the spice mixture on both sides.

Heat a large skillet over medium-high heat and add enough oil to coat the bottom of the pan.

Place the salmon in the pan and cook until the fish has cooked almost half-way through (2-3 minutes).

Flip and cook until the salmon is beginning to flake when poked with a skewer or metal fork (2-3 minutes).

Remove the fish to a plate and let rest for several minutes.

Wipe out the same pan and toast the buns quickly on both sides.

Assembly

Mix the wasabi and mayonnaise and taste. If the mixture is not spicy enough add another small dollop of wasabi.

Spread a heaping teaspoon of wasabi mayonnaise on the bottom bun and a light dollop on the top bun.

Lay a filet of salmon on the bottom bun and top with sliced tomatoes, onions, and a handful of arugula.

Enjoy with your favorite potato salad.

BAKLAVA

REDWOOD HEIGHTS, OAKLAND   PAVAN

There is a certain patience necessary when you begin to layer Baklava. You may find yourself cursing your little brush, which was supposed to effortlessly paint the butter onto the sheets of phyllo; or perhaps cursing yourself when you realize you forgot to defrost the phyllo dough. That is okay. You should remember that one of the excellent things about this recipe is that even with your small mistakes here and there, it will be doused with a honey syrup and it will be unfailingly delicious. Whether your cut diamonds of flaky goodness end up looking like circles, stop signs, or have no particular shape, don't worry; they will be eaten. Make sure you have enough to share.

PAVAN MADE BAKLAVA with her mother for the first time when she was ten. The dish has been passed down from her grandmother to her mother, and from her mother to her. In childhood, Pavan, her sister, and her parents lived on the first floor of their apartment building in Cambridge, Massachusetts. They were surrounded by relatives. Above them lived her grandfather, grandmother, and one of her uncles. On the same property lived an aunt, an uncle, and another five kids. On the top story of that house lived another aunt. Her mother's side of the family was a quick 20 minute drive away.

Some mornings Pavan would wake to the smell of roasting coffee coming from the floor above her—a smell she loved. On less fortunate days, the aroma of boiling lamb's head and braising brains would drift down through the vent in the ceiling. After school, she would go to the Greek Orthodox church, where the families of the neighborhood sent their children to learn Greek. Although Pavan's parents were not particularly religious, they wanted their children to learn their native language and culture.

Pavan was always surrounded by food. When she went upstairs to see her grandparents, her snacks often consisted of the buttons from the octopuses' tentacles, while the rest of the octopus stewed away on the stove. The smell of roasting bulbs

Some mornings Pavan would wake to the smell of roasting coffee coming from the floor above her—a smell she loved. On less fortunate days, the aroma of boiling lamb's head and braising brains would drift down through the vent in the ceiling...

of pungent garlic, or hot butter slowly sizzling at the bottom of a pan of baklava, form the memories of days spent in the kitchen with her mother and an extended family that loved to eat and cook.

After college, Pavan moved to San Francisco. Despite all her hours in the kitchen, it was only after she had finished school that she began to cook her own complete meals. The first thing she wanted to learn to make on her own was Pastitsio, a Greek alternative to lasagna, consisting of elbow macaroni and red meat sauce, topped off with a thick béchamel. For a long time after college, Pavan only cooked the things she had watched her mother cook and had been given the recipes for—Spanakopita, Pastitsio, Baklava, all the things that reminded her of home.

At law school in San Francisco, Pavan met Jim, her future husband. It was food that sparked their connection. For lunch, Pavan would bring increasingly elaborate Greek dishes she had cooked the night before, offering little bits of Spanakopita or Dolma to Jim at lunch. They sat together every day, enjoying the flavors of her Greek and his Italian cultures.

After they completed law school, San Francisco had become too expensive for them to consider buying a house there. Before they began their search for a home, Pavan had never spent any time in Oakland. When they were forced to expand their search and look outside San Francisco, she was surprised how beautiful Oakland was, and how much greenery and nature the city had to offer. She fell in love with the Glenview neighborhood, and that is where they began their family and had their two children. Redwood Heights, where they live now, is close to nature, but near enough to the recreation center, the schools, and the stores that it felt like a sensible place to move with kids when they outgrew their first house.

After 23 years living in Oakland, there are many places Jim and Pavan love. As the kids got older and then began to do their own things, Jim and Pavan discovered new areas of the city. Lake Merritt has become a favorite. It can be a challenge for this couple deciding where to eat. It could be a good night for Ikaros, a Greek restaurant on Grand Avenue, or maybe Ly Luck, a delicious Chinese restaurant on Fruitvale Avenue, right off of MacArthur Boulevard. If neither of those choices suit their mood, they might have dinner at Taqueria Los Comales on MacArthur Boulevard, or Nama Sushi on Fruitvale Avenue.

Stewed octopus and braised cow brains may not be on Pavan's dinner menu any more, but many childhood dishes certainly are. Forty-five years after Pavan first helped her mother brush melted butter on thin layers of phyllo and dust them with spiced sugar and nuts, she stands in her kitchen teaching the two of us. There is nothing quite like homemade Baklava, drenched in butter and honey syrup, sliced carefully into perfect diamonds, and rested overnight to help the flavors develop. If all you have ever tasted is store-bought Baklava, slightly soggy, dejected, and sweetened with corn syrup, this will be a very nice surprise. If you end up sharing with your friends, be prepared to make Baklava very often. Worse things could happen.

BAKLAVA

Yields 30-35 portions

Baklava requires a resting time of 8-24 hours before eating.

The phyllo should be defrosted in the refrigerator for 8-12 hours.

Baklava

½ cup sugar

2 teaspoons ground allspice

1 teaspoon ground cinnamon

1 teaspoon ground nutmeg

1 pound (4 cups) shelled walnuts, chopped finely or run through the food processor

2 sticks (8 ounces) sweet unsalted butter

1 pound phyllo dough

Cloves

Syrup

¾ cup water

1 ½ cups sugar

1 tablespoon honey

1 tablespoon lemon juice

DIRECTIONS

For the Baklava

Preheat the oven to 300 degrees.

Combine the sugar with the allspice, cinnamon, and nutmeg. Add walnuts and mix well. Melt the butter.

Brush the bottom of a 9 x 13 inch baking pan with a light layer of melted butter and place two folded sheets of phyllo in the pan. If the sheets do not fit nicely in the pan use a paring knife to cut them down to size. While you work, make sure to keep the phyllo sheets covered with a lightly dampened towel; otherwise the dough dries out and becomes fragile and brittle.

Brush the top layer of phyllo liberally and gently with butter so as not to tear it. Spread a thin layer of nut mixture over the phyllo; each nut layer gets about a ½ cup of nut mixture. Place another folded sheet in the pan, brush with butter but do not add nuts. It is okay if some layers of phyllo tear when they are being picked up; they can be pieced back together. Place another folded sheet, brush with butter, and spread a thin layer of nut mixture over the top. Continue to alternate between butter only and nut and butter layers until you have run out of nuts. Do not put butter or nuts on your final sheet of phyllo.

With a sharp knife, cut the pan of baklava lengthwise in 1-inch strips, then cut diagonally from one corner to the other through the middle of the pan. Continue cutting on this same diagonal, working from the middle outwards on both sides. This will create diamond shaped pieces. Before baking, place a clove in the top of each segment; they will serve as toothpicks and hold the pieces together nicely.

Dab one last liberal helping of butter over the top of each piece. Bake the Baklava for 1 hour, or until lightly browned.

Approximately 10 minutes before the Baklava is done, make the syrup.

For the syrup

In a small saucepan combine the water, sugar, honey, and lemon juice. Boil the mixture for ten minutes on medium heat. If the syrup is crystalizing and sticking to the sides of the pan add several more drops of lemon juice.

Once the Baklava is finished, pour the syrup evenly over the tray of Baklava.

Allow the Baklava to rest and absorb the syrup for 8-24 hours before arranging on a large platter and serving.

APPLE STRUDEL

MAXWELL PARK, OAKLAND   AMIE

Amie's strudel is not insanely sweet. Its flavor comes from the apples and raisins, which makes for a deliciously warming treat. You will understand when you get to the finishing point that this is almost like learning to fold a burrito, making sure all the apples and insides stay where they should be and the two ends meet. As you cut open the final product, steam will billow out, so pull some people around the cutting board to ooh and ahh in admiration.

RIGHT OFF HIGH STREET in the Maxwell Park neighborhood, Amie is surrounded by families running errands and businesses packed with people. Amie's apartment is a little oasis of peace and quiet in this lively part of town. Her shelves are filled with cookbooks written by every chef you may or may not have heard of. Her windows stay wide open above her cushy couch and the cool air pushes through the room and dances over the counters in the kitchen.

There are some people who are easy to love, and Amie is one of them. It may be her contagious smile. It may be the tattoos of flowers on one arm, or of whisk and measuring spoons wrapped with blue ribbons on her calves. Whatever it is that gets you, it is a good thing. And you will eat well in the process.

The way Amie gracefully moves through her kitchen as she teaches us to cook apple strudel, you would never guess she grew up in a household that was not big on home-cooked meals. In the seventies, Amie's mom worked and did not often have time to cook. By the time Amie was five or six, she was starting to do some of the cooking herself. Her mom would put all the cooking supplies low enough for her to reach them. Amie and her sister would make their own lunches every day.

Amie often eats her way across Oakland, trying the spices and flavors of every culture of the city…

Although Amie's family did not cook, the round wooden dinner table was the one place where the whole family congregated. And that same dinner table, covered in crayon markings and scratches from her childhood, is now nestled into Amie's Oakland home. Growing up, every night at six-thirty the whole family was expected to be at the dinner table. If Amie wanted to have a friend over for dinner, that was fine—five friends over, fine as well—as long as she made it to dinner. This is the same attitude Amie cooks with today. "I don't get out of bed for less then forty pounds of meat," she exclaimed with a warm laugh.

Amie grew up in Sacramento, then lived in Clear Lake, Sonoma, and Tahoe. She moved alone to San Francisco at 17 for college and after a year ended up in Oakland. Not long after she moved, her sister, still in high school, had a baby. By 19, Amie was taking care of her sister and nephew, working a full-time job at Peet's Coffee, and attending Mills College. The house she was sharing with her sister and nephew was too small and they moved to a new place, walking distance from work, a bus ride away from Mills College. Many of her friends were customers at Peet's and they all lived in her neighborhood. Amie and her friends began to cook dinners together.

Because Amie moved to Oakland so young, she has lived in nearly every neighborhood in the city—from Fruitvale to West Oakland to Temescal. Amie views all the change Oakland is now facing in a very positive light. She explained that in the time she has lived in Oakland, many of the notoriously underserved and dangerous neighborhoods have taken control of their own situations and beautified their surroundings.

Amie often eats her way across Oakland, trying the spices and flavors of every culture of the city. She fell in love with the Oaktown Spice Shop on Lakeshore, the Flora burger at Flora in Uptown, the donuts at Doughnut Dolly in Temescal, the colorful and spicy Indian food at Raj Indian Cuisine on Piedmont Avenue. But most of all she fell in love with the community she was able to create around her. Amie has formed a support system consisting of close friends and family, many of whom live within six blocks of her house.

If you decide it is a good night to make apple strudel or roast chicken or anything else, set an extra plate at the table and invite a friend because, as Amie would remind you, "You have your biological family and you have your logical family; food sculpts your logical family," a family made up of the people you trust and love.

APPLE STRUDEL

Yields 10 portions

Dough

2 ½ cups flour + more for dusting

¼ teaspoon salt

3 tablespoons + 1 teaspoon vegetable oil

1 cup lukewarm water

Filling

1 stick unsalted butter

⅛ cup bread crumbs

½ cup raisins

2 teaspoons lemon juice + ½ teaspoon zest

¾ cup + 1 tablespoon sugar

¼ teaspoon cinnamon

¼ teaspoon salt

⅓ cup toasted pecans, chopped finely

5-6 large Granny Smith or Gala apples (2 pounds), peeled, cored, cut into ½ inch cubes

DIRECTIONS

For forming the dough

Add the flour, salt, 3 tablespoons of the oil, and the warm water to a large bowl. Stir until the mixture is just combined. The dough should be shaggy but remain together when squeezed into a ball. If the mixture appears dry, add more water, one tablespoon at a time.

On a lightly floured surface, knead until the dough is smooth and slightly stretchy (3-5 minutes). Form the dough into a ball and coat with 1 teaspoon of the oil in a medium bowl. Cover with a dish towel for one hour. This will allow the flour in the dough to relax for the stretching to come.

For the filling and assembly

Melt 3 tablespoons of the butter in a small pan. Add the breadcrumbs and cook until the bread and butter smell toasty and have a little color on them. Set aside to cool.

Mix the raisins, lemon juice, and zest and allow the mixture to soak. In a separate small bowl combine ¾ cup of the sugar, cinnamon, and salt. Set aside.

Preheat the oven to 425 degrees.

Place a large sheet of parchment paper on your work surface and place a large kitchen towel on top. Roll out the dough on a lightly floured cutting board until it has formed a 10 by 12 inch rectangle. Carefully move the sheet of dough onto the towel.

Begin to carefully stretch the dough from the center out, trying to avoid tearing the dough. If the dough does tear you can patch it back together and continue stretching. Stretch the dough until it has

reached a size of 16 by 22 inches. The dough should be thin and see-through.

Melt the remaining butter and brush the dough generously. Set aside any extra butter to brush the formed strudel before it goes in the oven. Sprinkle chopped nuts over the dough, leaving a 5 inch border. Spread the bread crumb mixture over the far end of the dough in a 12 inch rectangle, 5 inches from the end of the dough and 2 inches from each side.

In a large bowl, combine the apples, raisin mixture, and the sugar. Place the apple mixture in a heaping pile on top of the breadcrumbs. Use your hands to push the apples down gently.

Lift the cloth from the side with the apples. Slowly lift the cloth higher and begin to roll the strudel. After the strudel has rolled one complete circle tuck in the edges and ensure no apple mixture has fallen out. Tuck the strudel tightly and continue to roll until there is no overhanging dough. The strudel will be a roll 12 to 14 inches long. Slide the strudel onto the parchment paper. Lift the paper and gently transfer the strudel to a baking sheet. Brush with the remaining butter and dust with the remaining tablespoon of sugar.

Bake for 20 minutes, then reduce the oven to 350 degrees. Continue to bake for 25-30 minutes, until the strudel is a light golden brown and the apples are tender.

Use two spatulas to carefully move the strudel to a cutting board and allow to cool.

Slice and serve with ice cream and whipped cream.

VEGAN CHOCOLATE CAKE

RANCHO SAN ANTONIO, OAKLAND   JADE

You will end up wanting to make this cake over and over, whether you are vegan or not. Since there are no eggs in the batter, you can eat as much of it as you want before pouring it into the cake pan. Just make sure enough is saved to fill the pan to the top, or maybe just make a recipe and a half.

JADE'S HOUSE ON EAST 19TH STREET is pushed back from the street, nestled between two taller buildings, like a magical house in an old story. The front door opens onto a staircase, winding upwards into a lofty living room and kitchen. We were welcomed by Jade's bright smile, complemented by her bright green hair. On the large unfinished wooden table in the middle of the shared kitchen and living room was everything Jade needed to make her vegan chocolate cake.

Jade has spent much of her life in the Rancho San Antonio neighborhood, with International Boulevard on one side and Fruitvale Avenue just a few minutes away. At a time when thousands of people are flocking to the city looking for a "cool new experience" and less expensive housing, Jade, at 17 and still in high school, has the perspective of a long-time resident. She has come to love and appreciate her neighborhood, but she assured us that has not always been the case.

"I grew up really thinking that where I lived wasn't the 'right' part of Oakland." In middle school, it was a struggle to connect with people who lived in a different part

*When she was younger,
eating dinner at taco
trucks and inexpensive
pho restaurants was an
embarrassment to Jade.
Eventually, though, all
that changed…*

of the city. Parents at her school were frightened about letting their children go to Jade's neighborhood. For years, the best option seemed to be to tell her classmates that she lived in the hills and that they simply could not come over because her room was messy.

When she was younger, eating dinner at taco trucks and inexpensive pho restaurants was an embarrassment to Jade. Eventually, though, all that changed. The city around her began to come to life for Jade. "With accepting my house and neighborhood, I've been able to accept parts of myself I wasn't able to before." Jade credited much of this change in her attitude to a local company called Oaklandish, an Oakland lifestyle and clothing brand which supports local charities and cultivates Oakland pride. It may seem strange to think that t-shirts and hoodies could change attitudes, but Oaklandish helped her see Oakland in a different light.

There is sadness in Jade's voice as she goes on to speak about what she perceives as the lack of appreciation by some of the newcomers for what is truly special in her neighborhood. A shift has begun. People are not integrating into the culture that has already been created in her neighborhood. Many of the newcomers are moving in and aiming to create their own closed-off communities.

For Jade, one of the great things about her neighborhood is how many cultures intersect. She lives next to a Salvadorian couple who speak little English, but never refrain from coming to Jade's house with smiles and sandwiches stacked high with turkey. Across the street lives a couple from Guam who make jams out of fruits Jade can never identify, and knit scarves for their dog, Tolstoy.

Although Jade sees a change in her neighborhood that worries her, she still sees many places in the city that remain the same. "My favorite place, I think, would be San Antonio Park," walking distance from her house. She also advised anyone in the area to check out Taqueria San Jose, off of International Boulevard. It has not yet been discovered by hipsters, and the patio is adorned with paintings of Jesus and the Virgin Mary. Champa Garden is another favorite, a restaurant where many of the Laotian families in the neighborhood gather. Jade says the long wait is worth it for the incredible food.

As we talked, flour drifted through the air, sugar and cocoa powder were sifted, and coconut oil melted on a low heat, forming a rich batter. Enjoy Jade's cake by the spoonful, or bake it for a special someone's birthday. Next time you run out of eggs or butter, there is hope.

VEGAN CHOCOLATE CAKE

Yields 12-14 slices

Batter

1 package (2 ¼ teaspoons) yeast

¾ cup warm water

1 ½ cups cake flour

1 teaspoon baking soda

1 teaspoon baking powder

1 cup organic sugar

½ teaspoon salt

5 tablespoons coconut oil

1 tablespoon vanilla extract

1 tablespoon apple cider vinegar

½ cup unsweetened cocoa powder

5 ounces semisweet (vegan) chocolate chips or finely chopped pieces

Frosting

1 ½ cups peanut butter (smooth, unsweetened)

1 ⅓ cups coconut cream

1 ½ tablespoons agave

2 teaspoons salt

DIRECTIONS

For the batter

Preheat the oven to 350 degrees.

In a large bowl, combine the yeast and water and let stand until foamy (about 10 minutes).

Mix the the flour, baking soda, baking powder, sugar, and salt.

Add the coconut oil, vanilla extract, and apple cider vinegar to the yeast mixture and whisk to combine.

Sift the dry ingredients into the wet. Sift the cocoa powder into the batter and fold to incorporate. Mix the chocolate chunks into the batter.

Cut a piece of parchment paper to fit into the bottom of a 9 inch cake pan and pour the batter into the pan, gently spreading with a rubber spatula.

Bake the cake for 20 minutes and test for doneness. Shake the cake pan very gently; if the batter has not yet set on the outside rim, cook for 5-7 more minutes until the center of the cake shakes very gently but the outside rim has set.

Flip the cake onto a cutting board or serving platter, peel off the parchment paper, and allow to cool.

For the frosting

Combine the peanut butter, coconut cream, agave, and salt, and whisk vigorously until light and creamy. Taste for balance before frosting the cake.

Serve with vegan ice cream.

RESOURCES

Abura-Ya (380 15th St., Oakland)
Japanese fried chicken and beer garden.

Asmara Restaurant (5020 Telegraph Ave., Oakland)
Well-decorated space serves up fresh and genuine Ethiopian/
Eritrean cuisine.

Aunt Mary's Cafe (4640 Telegraph Ave, Oakland)
Breakfast and lunch, offers a cozy neighborhood spot with a
Southern influence.

B-Dama (907 Washington St., Oakland)
Traditional Japanese fare in historic Swan's Marketplace.

Ba Le Vietnamese Sandwich (1909 International Blvd., Oakland)
Counter service and generously stuffed Vietnamese sandwiches.

Baja Taqueria (4070 Piedmont Ave., Oakland)
Vibrant interior with a freshly prepared Mexican menu.

Boot & Shoe Service (3308 Grand Ave., Oakland)
Thin crust pizzas, cocktails, and delicious sandwiches.

Cafe Eritrea D'Afrique (4069 Telegraph Ave., Oakland)
Small Eritrean cafe conveniently located above Macarthur BART.
Specializes in traditional stews, platters, and honey wine.

Cam Huong (920 Webster St., Oakland)
Vietnamese sandwich shop serves heaping sandwiches, with
friendly service.

Camino (3917 Grand Ave., Oakland)
Rustic Californian cuisine, mostly cooked in one of the two
wood-burning ovens.

Champa Garden (2102 8th Ave., Oakland)
Laotian fusion restaurant offering a delicious array of dishes.
Quick service and friendly atmosphere.

Colonial Donuts (3318 Lakeshore Ave., Oakland)
A staple for fresh doughnuts in Oakland, open 24 hours a day.

Commis (3859 Piedmont Ave., Oakland)
New American fixed price menu offers Michelin experience.
Deliciously fresh ingredients and excellent service.

Cybelle's (3762 Piedmont Ave., Oakland)
Large pizza slices and quick delivery.

**Doughnut Dolly (482 B 49th St., Oakland & 1313 9th St.,
Berkeley)**
Artisan hand-crafted doughnuts filled with a selection of classic
and unusual fillings.

Duende (468 19th St., Oakland)
Upscale and beautifully designed space serves tapas, large
plates, and artfully created paellas.

Ensarro Ethiopian Restaurant (357 Grand Ave., Oakland)
Serves up delicious Ethiopian dishes from their new location,
across the street from the old spot. Freshly made Injera and beers
on tap.

Flora (1900 Telegraph Ave., Oakland)
Serves up reinvented American classics and delicious cocktails in an Art Deco space.

Guadalajara Taco Truck (44th Ave. and International Blvd., Oakland)
Taco truck offers burritos as well. Pinned by many "best taco truck in Oakland."

Hawker Fare (2300 Webster St., Oakland & 680 Valencia St., San Francisco)
Thai street food in a lively and energetic space.

Ikaros Greek Restaurant (3268 Grand Ave., Oakland)
Greek restaurant serves family style Greek meals inspired by the dishes of Ikaria Island.

Iyasare (1830 Fourth St., Berkeley)
Minimalist space serves up inventive dishes from northeast Japan as well as nigiri and sashimi.

Kamdesh Afghan Kabab House (332 14th St., Oakland)
Dimly lit and loved by locals, offers a variety of traditional Afghan dishes.

Koryo Jajang (4390 Telegraph Ave., Oakland)
Traditional Korean fare located in the Koryo Village Plaza.

Little Shin Shin (4258 Piedmont Ave., Oakland)
Chinese restaurant serving Hunan, Szechuan, and Mandarin cuisine. Friendly service and fresh ingredients.

Ly Luck (3537 Fruitvale Ave., Oakland)
Chinese food in a casual environment.

Nama Sushi (3400 Fruitvale Ave., Oakland)
Beautifully presented sushi, a neighborhood establishment.

Penrose (3311 Grand Ave., Oakland)
Beautiful high-ceilinged restaurant serves a taste of North Africa. Large communal tables and modern bar.

Peony Seafood Restaurant (388 9th St., #288, Oakland)
Large, busy, Chinese restaurant. Serves dim sum and Cantonese dishes.

Pizzaiolo (5008 Telegraph Ave., Oakland)
Seasonal Italian fare from the wood oven.

Raj Indian Cuisine (4086 Piedmont Ave., Oakland)
Delicious and crisp Indian flavors.

Ruby King Bakery Cafe (718 Franklin St., Oakland)
Inexpensive, freshly baked Chinese pastries. The cocktail bun is highly recommended.

Taqueria Los Comales (2105 MacArthur Blvd., Oakland)
Vibrant interior with a freshly prepared Mexican menu.

Taqueria San Jose (3433 International Blvd., Oakland)
Deliciously fresh Mexican food at a very reasonable price.

The Dock at Linden Street (95 Linden St., Oakland)
Delicious New American fare and cocktails served in the industrial section of the city.

Wood Tavern (6317 College Ave., Oakland)
Rustic space offers California-inspired sustainable fare and wines.

Xyclo (4218 Piedmont Ave., Oakland)
Upscale Vietnamese restaurant serves fresh and seasonal dishes. Vietnamese-inspired cocktails as well.

MARKETS

Berkeley Bowl (920 Heinz Ave., Berkeley & 2020 Oregon St., Berkeley)
Offers a massive selection of organic and natural produce, and many hard-to-find ingredients.

Euromix (4301 Piedmont Ave. #C, Oakland)
Small neighborhood market provides a variety of European specialty items.

Farmer Joe's Marketplace (3501 MacArthur Blvd., Oakland & 3426 Fruitvale Ave., Oakland)
Neighborhood grocery store offers organic and natural produce.

Mi Pueblo Food Center (1630 High St., Oakland)
Latin supermarket stocks meat, seafood, produce, and specialty items.

Mi Tierra Foods (2082 San Pablo Ave., Oakland)
Mexican grocery store sells fresh masa for tortillas as well as a variety of dried spices. Boasts a reasonably sized produce section as well as meat and a bakery.

New Hop Lung Meat Market (878 Webster St., Oakland)
Provides fresh produce as well as variety of meats. Meat can be ground on request.

99 Ranch Market (3288 Pierce St. #99, Richmond)
Asian supermarket supplies imported specialty items as well as meat, seafood, produce, and baked goods.

Oaktown Spice Shop (546 Grand Ave., Oakland)
High quality spices, herbs, and blends.

Ras Dashen Market (5831 Telegraph Ave., Oakland)
Ethiopian/Eritrean grocer, supplies limited but high quality ingredients. Spice blends made in house by family.

Riverdog Farm (Tuesday and Saturday Farmers Markets, Berkeley)
Organic local produce at a reasonable price. Also sells highly coveted eggs by the half or full dozen and responsibly raised meat.

MISCELLANEOUS

Berkeleyside (berkeleyside.com)
Berkeley's independent news site.

Girls Inc. of Alameda County (510 16th St., Oakland)
Nonprofit focuses on giving confidence and resources to girls.

Oaklandish (1444 Broadway Ave., Oakland & 3419 Fruitvale Ave., Oakland)
Local fashion line promotes civic pride and highlights the Oakland logo.

Oakland Tribune
Oakland's newspaper of record, providing news for the surrounding area.

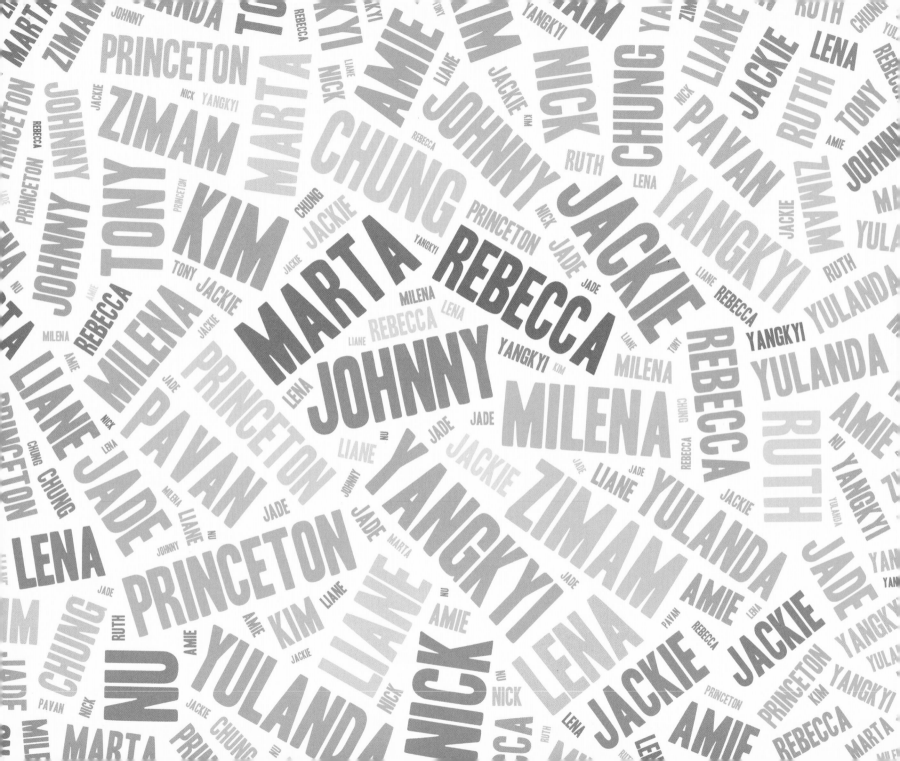